5.76

D0914814

DATE DUE

Toward Strategies for Public Administration
Development in Latin America

Toward Strategies for Public Administration Development in Latin America

JOHN C. HONEY

With Commentaries by
PETER D. BELL,
RICHARD A. FEHNEL,
JAMES R. HIMES, *and*
GEORGE SUTIJA

SYRACUSE UNIVERSITY PRESS

Copyright © 1968 by Syracuse University Press
Syracuse, New York

FIRST EDITION

MANUFACTURED IN THE UNITED STATES OF AMERICA

Foreword

Writers on development problems have often been accused of excluding Latin America, of thinking exclusively in terms of Asia and Africa. Perhaps we have learned to think so much in terms of great cultural areas and geographic regions, and the drama involved in the postwar struggles for independence which led in recent years to the proliferation of new states, that we have become preoccupied with the Afro-Asian segments of the "third world." We should therefore be grateful to John C. Honey for preparing this important study on the problems Latin American countries face in their efforts to improve administrative capabilities in relation to developmental needs.

Readers whose chief concern has been with problems of economic, political, or administrative development in the areas south or east of Suez will find much to interest them. For example, prevalence of military rule in many of these Asian and African lands has its counterparts in the Western Hemisphere. One is inclined to think that the frequency of military coups d'état in developing countries does not reflect a cultural idiosyncrasy of any religious, linguistic, or racial population but rather a syndrome which recurs, almost predictably, whenever the new political institutions of government—political parties, legislatures, and elected executives—prove too weak to control bureaucracies, both military and political, in which the expansive forces of modernization express themselves as the needs of a service-oriented state replace earlier conceptions of law and order regimes. Under these circumstances inter- or intra-bureaucratic struggles become the dominant form of political action, and it is scarcely surprising that military officers should be able to overcome their unarmed counterparts in the civilian bureaucracies.

Another problem of universal relevance to development is the degree to which balance is required between what might, at times, seem to be mutually opposed tendencies. On the one hand there is need for increased productivity in the economy and for greater efficiency in governmental operations. Authoritarian and single-party regimes have often claimed that they could perform these functions more effectively if they did not have to contend with interference by popular movements and representative bodies. On the other hand, the demand for more equitable distribution of goods and services, for more democratic forms of government and greater social justice, have also been heard in the developing countries. The insistence of once colonial peoples on independence, regardless of economic cost, demonstrates the widespread popularity of equalitarian norms. Hopefully, a highly developed political and economic system would be able to satisfy both the demand for economic growth and for democratization. But can these two goals be satisfied simultaneously in developing countries? Must a given society tend to favor one at the expense of the other? The experience of Latin America during the last century provides an illuminating test case when viewed against the background of events in Asia and Africa since the last war.

For problems such as these to be solved in Asia, the Middle East, and Africa, as in Latin America, much more needs to be known about the current situation, the interrelationships of social forces, of political and administrative behavior, of economic forces and cultural systems. In many of these matters we are inadequately informed. Professor Honey rightly calls attention to the need for basic research, for data collection and analysis, in Latin America —a need which is equally great elsewhere. The obstacles to such research, and to the dissemination of relevant knowledge already available, are similar outside of Latin America, and proposals made here for strengthening educational and research programs and for creating appropriate machinery for international cooperation could well be adapted to the situation in other continents.

Too much of the research which has been carried on by "area specialists" and social scientists studying the characteristics and development problems of the various countries and peoples of the third world has tended to omit consideration of the bureaucracies of government and the operations of public administration. Family systems, language and religion, economic conditions and politics—such seem to have been the attractive and popular subjects of study. Yet all of these problems are affected by governmental activities and capabilities, and all of them, in turn, influence the norms and capabilities of governmental bureaucracies. Honey's work directs attention to these administrative dimensions of development in Latin America, a focus of attention which is equally relevant and necessary for other parts of the developing world.

Policy makers and the public in the United States tend, all too often, to think of the "non-Western" world in terms of broad stereotypes, lumping together phenomena which often, on closer inspection, turn out to be highly dissimilar. Certainly even an area which at first might sound quite homogeneous, such as Southeast Asia, is actually very heterogeneous. The underlying Sinic influences in Indochina are quite different from the Indic influences which prevail in Thailand, Burma, and Indonesia. The American and Spanish influences in the Philippines have produced responses very different from the responses to the French influence in Vietnam or the British in Malaysia and Burma. Insular Southeast Asia differs from the peninsular countries, the urban centers from the rural hinterlands, the densely packed valleys from the sparsely settled hill country. Honey draws attention to comparable differences which make generalizations about Latin America equally risky and misleading.

In this context the need for more research and information becomes apparent. It is encouraging to observe the new policies and leadership of the Agency for International Development; this Agency plans to invest funds to help develop greater institutional resources and capabilities in American universities instead of merely utilizing the meager and perhaps dwindling stockpile of resources previously built up. The new program authorized by the International Education Act will, it may be hoped, also reinforce this enrichment of our intellectual and institutional resources. Perhaps the large private foundations will continue, as they have in the past, to support the strengthening of research and teaching capabilities in our universities as regards the problems of development, including the administrative problems of the third world. Honey calls attention to these problems as they affect Latin America, and such needs are compelling for other areas of the world as well.

The need exists also to establish new patterns of cooperation among American intellectuals and scholarly institutions and their counterparts in the developing countries. International bodies such as UNESCO, the foundations, and governmental programs enhance such efforts, but much remains to be done. It is to be hoped that Honey's recommendations for Latin America will be implemented and that equally forward-looking programs can be launched elsewhere.

The book which follows is to be commended especially to readers interested in Latin America, but those who are interested in comparative and development administration, indeed with development in general, will also find much worth considering.

Palo Alto, California   FRED W. RIGGS
November, 1967

Preface

The practical experiences and intellectual interests underlying this essay go back a good many years. Shortly after World War II, I had an opportunity, while a visiting professor in the Graduate School of Public Administration, University of Puerto Rico, to consult with the Insular government on the establishment of a new merit system for public employees. In the course of this work my curiosity was aroused by the fact that this was the fourth effort to set up a merit system in Puerto Rico since the island had become associated with the United States. I wondered what forces had been at play in Puerto Rican society which militated against the success of the first three attempts; what characteristics of these "U.S. Made" merit systems, had been uncongenial to the Puerto Rican environment? A further source of curiosity was that this latest attempt seemed to be taking hold, leading to speculation that the situation in Puerto Rico might now be receptive to an administrative system designed essentially for a modern, industrial society.

More than a decade later, just about the time the Alliance for Progress was coming into existence, the Institute of Public Administration, New York, was asked to consult with USAID and the government of Peru on measures which might be instituted to strengthen that country's public administration. Since I was serving as deputy director of the Institute, the task fell principally to me. It was almost immediately evident that a significantly different set of forces was at work in the Peruvian environment than I had encountered before. The cultures of Peru, its geographic diversity, its powerful colonial heritage, and many other factors set it distinctively apart from every other country even including its close neighbors in South America. It was also soon clear that Peru's first governmental problems were hardly the installation of a merit system, or the establishment of more effective budgetary procedures, much as these might be needed. Its first problems were related to maintenance of constitutional government, the generation of responsible legislative behavior, and the development of sound priorities among the myriad of requirements for modernization. Under these circumstances the traditional definition of public administration, as governmental staff services, lost significance.

Subsequent opportunities to look at governmental problems in Venezuela and in such diverse countries as Egypt, the East African states of Uganda, Kenya, and Tanzania, India, and Maylasia tended to confirm earlier speculations about the significance of culture and environment for public administration, and about its scope. Discussions with colleagues at the Institute of Public Administration, New York, and with officials in the USAID Latin American Program first stimulated the question of whether it might be possible to frame strategies for public administration development. As one AID official said: "We have strategies for agricultural development; we're moving toward strategies for educational development. Is it possible to do this for public administration?"

The generosity of the Ford Foundation, and in particular of its Latin American Program, allowed me to explore the public administration strategies question while serving the Foundation in a consulting capacity. I am particularly indebted to Harry Wilhelm, director of the Latin American Program, and to John Hilliard and Reynolds Carlson, former associate directors of the Program, for their interest and encouragement. Virtually all of the Foundation's Latin American field staff provided advice and assistance during the course of the inquiry.

In the several months devoted to this effort I talked with numerous Latin American officials both in the United States and in their own countries. Such interviews were invaluable and indeed essential. I also talked extensively with officials of international agencies and with university colleagues in a number of institutions. All such assistance is acknowledged with appreciation.

The four analyses which accompany my essay and which relate it to the current situation in Brazil, Chile, Peru, and Venezuela were prepared, on their own initiative, by Peter D. Bell, of the Ford Foundation's staff in Brazil; Richard A. Fehnel, of Cornell University, formerly a Ford Foundation fellow in Chile; James R.

Himes, of the Ford Foundation staff in Peru; and George Sutija, of the Ford Foundation staff in Venezuela. Their observations are astute and unofficial.

During the preparation of this work I was fortunate to have the research assistance of Allan Austin, of the Institute of Public Administration, New York. In particular, Mr. Austin prepared the materials on the programs of the agencies, external to Latin America, which are involved in public administration development.

It is my hope that the approaches suggested in the following pages may be stimulating to government and university officials in the various countries of Latin America. It is they who bear the most immediate responsibilities for the modernization of their nations. While the ideas and procedures we propose are hardly simple, and certainly will be only partially relevant in any specific setting, they stem from the same deep concern with modernization that animates their prospective audience.

It is my further hope that those who are concerned with assisting Latin American public administration development from the outside—foundation officials and personnel in the international and inter-American organizations and in USAID—may find some merit in what I have to say. Whether merit is to be found or not, the author must accept full responsibility.

New York City
August, 1967   JOHN C. HONEY

Contents

Toward Strategies for Public Administration
Development in Latin America

I

Introduction

Skill in the arts of public administration is often regarded as a resource of economically developed countries such as the United States and Great Britain and as an attribute which must be acquired by most countries currently going through the processes of modernization. But in fact even the so-called advanced countries are constantly grappling with administrative change and development, especially during periods of crisis or when major shifts in governmental activities occur. Vice President Hubert Humphrey noted in late 1965 that the great challenge for the United States in the years ahead would be in generating the capacity and skill to administer the many programs of the Great Society which Congress had recently approved.

If this is true for the United States, the far more demanding tasks of modernization such as agricultural reform, industrial development, improvement of housing and health conditions, and the extension of literacy impose enormous burdens on the governments of Latin America. Public administration is unavoidably involved since only governments can muster the power and resources to effect major socio-economic change. In the absence of governmental initiative and leadership, development is almost certain to be fragmentary and episodic.

Definitions of public administration vary considerably. A commonly held view is that public administration is the bureaucratic aspect of government, the central permanent machinery of the state which conducts the public business. However, as one reflects on the complexities of modernization it becomes evident that governments must be concerned with more than the competence of their bureaucracies. For example, for several nations in Latin America the first order of business in recent years has been to maintain constitutional government, to effect orderly transitions from one legally established regime to the next, and to keep po-

litical extremism under reasonable control. Only as there is progress in these "first order" matters is it possible to get on with the
reforms and developments which constitute modernization.

Thus, for our purposes public administration is taken to be the
processes of government in their totality. Such matters as political
leadership, the nature and functions of political parties, and constitutional structures are all elements of a country's public administration. The citizenry itself—how it views government, responds to
governmental leadership, and assumes responsibilities for and in
government—is a vital factor in any system of public administration. So, also, is the whole complex of institutions for public law
enactment and enforcement, for the performance of these institutions influences citizen attitudes toward government, and it is these
institutions which contribute to making government responsive or
indifferent to the requirements of modernization. Legislatures, as
the generators of laws which provide authority, as well as the
requisite resources for modernization, are also a critical part of
the public administration process. These elements at the central
governmental level have their counterparts in the political sub-
divisions of the nation. All contribute to the system of public administration.

The objective here is to suggest strategies which may assist in
strengthening the public administration processes in the countries
of Latin America. I have considered the problem at large, and with
broad implementing approaches, instead of attempting to establish
a rigorous pattern of steps to be followed in particular situations.
Recognizing that the formulation of intra-country strategies is
primarily the task of leaders in each country, I have made proposals as suggestions to be explored rather than formulas to be
applied.

This is quite precisely the approach taken by the authors of the
commentaries on Brazil, Chile, Peru, and Venezuela. Against a
background of interest in public administration development, and
a substantial knowledge of the history, cultures, economics, and
governmental institutions of the countries about which they write,
they have drawn upon the strategies proposals in a selective
manner and have given their views on the necessary and feasible
next steps. But as at least one of the authors has pointed out, the
task of developing an intra-country strategy also requires an inti-
mate assessment of the current political situation and of available

financial resources which might be directed to public administration problems. Thus the basic task comes back to the leadership in individual countries.

In my opinion the most favorable condition for any nation is one in which the citizenry controls the selection of political leaders. The precise form of government, whether presidential, parliamentary, or otherwise, is far less significant than is the assurance of popular participation. Moreover, government must function through the rule of law, or the capacity of the citizen to participate will soon be eroded. The public administration of countries operating under the rule of law, with participant citizenries, is bound to be different from public administration in countries in which the instruments of government are otherwise selected.

The play of nationalism upon economic and social forces produces problems in many of the modernizing nations in Latin America as well as elsewhere. Imperatives difficult to understand and control lead to a variety of extra-legal governments. Scholars lack full understanding of the relationships between development and the various parts of representative government, e.g., the relationship among political parties, efficient bureaucratic systems, and the processes of development. Chaos can exist within governments chosen by popular vote just as progress can exist under military juntas and one-party systems.

Future efforts to develop the systems of public administration in Latin America must be experimental and pragmatic. It is certain that substantial practical measures must be undertaken to deal with urgent current problems. We cannot afford to wait for research to clarify the wisest routes. But at the same time we cannot afford, either, to move solely with current demands in mind. To do this would leave us in a perennial state of relative ignorance. Thus strategies will be proposed which are relevant to the present; others are designed to increase knowledge concerning how to proceed in the future.

There has been on the part of some scholars and officials an erroneous disposition to find and focus on a single key to development in Latin America. But it is nearly as fallacious to suppose that social and economic development in Latin America will follow on primary concentration of attention to public administration as to presume that population control, increased food production, or opening up the heartland of the continent provides the key solution. Development must move apace on many fronts. If there is an "art" to development, it may be found, perhaps, in devoting balanced attention to key interrelated elements.

A tendency exists, frequently encouraged by political considerations, to see modernization as a goal, the achievement of which is just around the bend; the metaphorical bend may be the next presidential term or the next decade. This inclination exists among observers in Latin America and the United States. Nor are members of the external and regional assisting organizations immune. Numerous efforts have been made to identify the steps in the modernization process and to suggest at what stages nations can "go it alone"; while the products of these efforts can be interesting and useful, erroneous implications may result from them. Two fallacious notions are apparent: first, that properly designed and applied programs of financial and technical assistance will bring each nation to the point, in the near future, where is can be "cut loose"; second, that there is a kind of static quality to the condition of modernization which eliminates the need for continuing external associations.

The processes of modernization are extremely complex, involving fundamental value changes in society, and the points at which modernization will be complete are impossible to identify. Indeed, the economic and social interdependence of nations strongly suggests that the Alliance for Progress will be a more or less permanent arrangement, its programs changing to accommodate the conditions which emerge both in Latin America and in the United States. Particularly with respect to public administration, innovation and experimentation are necessary; they are aided by contact with the experience of other countries.

The supporting agencies' practice of markedly varying the amount of their assistance to particular countries on the basis of short-term considerations stems in part from their narrow view of the modernization process and their natural desire to see and display results. Plunging in and out of technical assistance programs is costly and inefficient, however. The sense of balance and poise that is called for can be realized only if it is encouraged and practiced at the highest leadership levels both in Latin America and in the various assisting institutions.

There is need for continuous adaptation and exchanges of experience in public administration if governmental processes are to serve the purposes of development. Interests in both the developed and modernizing countries can be advanced through such exchanges. First in the intellectual sphere, so to speak, some of the outstanding developments in political science and public administration in the United States have derived from the opportunity which scholars and practitioners have had to work abroad, particularly in the modernizing countries. The explorations now under way into citizen values—how they are shaped and how they influence and are influenced by the governmental processes—the relationships between administrative practices and political stability, and the influence of bureaucracy on economic and social development are illustrative. Such inquiries are illuminating issues of importance for all countries, modernizing or otherwise.

At the practical level, it may simply be noted, by way of illustration, that assistance in establishing straightforward and clear procedures for the launching of new businesses is one of the means whereby public administration technical assistance can serve both the modernizing government and foreign investors.

The final point is that the field of public administration, being as broad in scope as it is, can tolerate, indeed needs, many centers and resources of initiative. This is not to urge an uncoordinated proliferation of training, research, and technical assistance institutions. But a great variety of talent is required: the generalist policy maker; the legal expert; the functionally specialized administrator; the broad-gauged administrative manager; the administrative technician trained in finance, accounting, and organization and methods; and the municipal administrator. Developing the requisite cadres of such personnel will demand full use of the resources of universities, public administration institutes, schools, and in-service training programs. Programs of foreign study, whether in the United States or elsewhere, should also preferably involve the use of a number of institutions. Public administration is both too varied and too lacking in intellectual unity to warrant the exposure of one modernizing country to only one external institution's outlook.

II

Current Approaches to
Public Administration Development

The countries of Latin America have concerned themselves with some aspects of public administration development, on their own initiative, for a number of years. Included in this chapter are illustrative examples of such "self-help" as well as a review of some of the programs of leading external institutions which provide assistance in public administration and related areas.

COUNTRY APPROACHES

While generalizations about the state of public administration in Latin America have limited utility, some of the more or less common characteristics are suggested here to illustrate the setting for measures taken by several of the governments.

The prestige of the public service is generally low throughout the Southern Hemisphere. While holding elective office or presidential appointment is honorific, there is little respect for lower level, working government officials and only slightly more for senior, permanent officials. Pay scales are correspondingly poor. As a consequence, many civil servants work at more than one job, the second outside of government, ordinarily. While some countries have good civil service legislation on the books, a civil service system which is operating and widely respected, such as in Great Britain, France, or the United States, scarcely exists. Political connections often determine selection. In 1962 it was claimed by knowledgable observers that to be considered for a governmental position in Peru one needed ten political endorsements.

Well-established standards for recruitment exist for only a few positions. In Latin America as a whole there is a great shortage of well-trained professional people; this shortage is even greater in the public service. The national legislative bodies have so little staff assistance that informed action is difficult. The offices of presidents are similarly poorly equipped in all the countries except Brazil. Below the national level, the resources, taxing authority, and legal mandate to develop vigorous decentralized government are lacking. State and local government personnel are even more scarce and ill trained than those in the federal or national hierarchies.

The Venezuelan government has recently taken more formal measures than perhaps any other to improve its public administration. In an attempt to strengthen the image of the public service and to establish a body to improve the public administration of the nation, it created the Public Administration Commission. The Commission, which began its life with a distinguished membership, has unfortunately lost ground both in prestige and political influence in recent years. Venezuela's School of Public Administration has concentrated its efforts on two programs: (1) in-service training courses for semi-skilled administrative personnel, and (2) a school diploma program for management employees who have not completed secondary school. Private interests are now drawing up plans for a new Advanced School of Administration which will offer training to both business and government executives.

Attempting to strengthen the municipalities, the national government created the Foundation for Community Development and Municipal Improvement in 1962. The chief function of the Foundation is to provide funds and technical help to Venezuela's cities and towns. A research institute, CENDES, operates within the framework of CORDIPLAN, Venezuela's planning agency. Currently, CENDES is conducting studies designed to increase knowledge of the political framework in Venezuela.

Brazil has long tried to improve its public administration system, and the national government has introduced a new program of administrative reform. If this program is successful, there will be created a senior civil service and a staff college for training higher civil servants. Under the program, an attempt is also being made to relate the budgeting and planning functions to each other more effectively than has been done in the past. An Administrative Reform Commission under outstanding leadership is guiding these efforts. Evidence of Brazil's concern with public administration training is found in the more than twenty training programs and institutes throughout the country. Two of the most influential are the Brazilian School of Public Administration, sponsored by the Getúlio Vargas Foundation, and the Brazilian Institute of Municipal Administration.

In Peru public administration development was for many years in a quiescent state. The government maintained, but with limited financial support, the Peruvian Institute of Public Administration (IPAP) within the Ministry of Justice. Under the impact of political changes within Peru and because of prompting from the Alliance for Progress, the government revitalized the Institute and placed it within the Office of the Presidency in close association with the National Planning Organization. Now known as the National Office of Rationalization and Training in Public Administration (ONRAP), the body has responsibility for training and administrative reform in the government. Its leadership maintains close ties with the Presidency; it works cooperatively with the National Planning Institute, attempting to diagnose public administrative problems that inhibit the execution of established plans. ONRAP is seeking, through use of its own staff as well as external assistance, to deal with certain of these problems. The national office is now firmly established, and it is strategically placed in the governmental framework. The results ONRAP is achieving are illustrative of strong political support for administrative improvement.

Chile has fewer problems of corruption in its public administration system than most of the other countries. Its public service, however, is overstaffed; productivity is low. Indicative of these conditions is the fact that between 70 and 80 per cent of the government's budget is allocated for the salaries of public employees. Currently efforts are being made, under the leadership of the director of the national budget, to increase productivity and achieve greater management efficiency in selected strategic organizations such as the universities, the Ministries of Health and Transport, and the Post Office. The government is also attempting to improve the management of its purchasing system and statistical services and of the Ministry of Public Works.

While these illustrations of country efforts in public administration do not tell the entire story, they illustrate the types of activities which to a greater or lesser degree can be found in many of the Latin American nations.

AGENCY FOR INTERNATIONAL DEVELOPMENT (AID)

AID strategies for the development of public administration are "country" strategies, generally intended to improve administrative deficiencies and shortcomings identified by the AID staff in its analyses of individual countries. After identifying the areas of weakness, AID prepares programs and projects to meet problems in those areas in which the host government is willing to cooperate. Little evolvement of general strategy for public administration development has occurred, though attention has been devoted to the improvement of tax systems and to fiscal affairs generally. The United States Internal Revenue Service, for example, has assisted AID by providing technicians and training for tax programs.

The development of strategy is retarded because major portions of the effort to improve administrative capacities do not fall within the jurisdiction of its Division of Development Administration, which is nominally responsible for administrative development within the Office of Institutional Development. Education, for example, is a priority area. Both in its technical assistance and loan activities AID tries to improve educational administration. AID activity takes place, however, without the participation of the Division. To a lesser extent, the same is true in agriculture, where administrative reforms are carried out by members of agricultural field parties. AID generally grants its loans to operations that stress development of institutional, including administrative, competence, rather than to organizations in the process of building roads, schools, sewers, etc. AID lends a large portion of its funds through public lending agencies, and today the Agency is giving greater attention to strengthening the administrative capacity of these institutions to carry out their programs.

Within AID's Development Administration Division, country

programs are formulated with the collaboration of either AID public administration advisers or representatives of contracting institutions. The contract method of developing country programs in public administration was designed partially to offer greater flexibility in recruitment and operations than was formerly possible.

Illustrative AID country programs are:

Brazil. A great deal of public administration training and technical assistance activity is undertaken by the Brazilian government assisted by AID. The Brazilian government has prepared a major administrative reform program. AID, for its part, has placed high priority on public administration in its planning and is developing broad programs for administrative support of development activities, designed to complement the activities of the government.

Argentina. Given the unique nature of United States-Argentinian relationships, the AID program has been particularly concerned with finding mutually acceptable modes of operation. Programs include an Internal Revenue Service tax team working with the national tax office, general accounting office personnel engaged in the introduction of program budgeting, and the training of personnel for implementation of a program budget. AID is presently developing a program for budget training in cooperation with the United States Federal Bureau of the Budget, the New York State Bureau of the Budget, and the Tennessee Valley Authority.

Chile. Although not a great deal is being done by AID in the field of public administration, initiative is being taken by the Chilean government. AID activities have tended to emphasize specific, technical projects, such as a tax study completed in the mid-1960's.

Peru. AID activities in public administration have developed from a series of courses in records management, supervised by a direct-hire AID technician, to the present multi-faceted program of teaching, consulting, and research being conducted at ONRAP through a contract group, the Institute of Public Administration in New York. Substantial work has also been done in the fields of tax and customs administration.

FORD FOUNDATION

The Ford Foundation characteristically works through educational institutions both at home and abroad. It has tended to emphasize the development of the social sciences in Latin American universities as the means of strengthening the intellectual foundations of applied activities such as public administration.

Training and Research in Latin America. The Ford Foundation has sought strategic opportunities for strengthening public administration training and research; increasingly, its efforts have been directed toward strengthening the basic social sciences. Representative activities closely related to public administration have included the support of training and research in institutes such as the Instituto Superior de Administración Pública (ISAP) in Argentina and in the Escola Superior de Administración Pública (EBAP) in Brazil.

A grant in 1966 to the Federal University of Minas Gerais, in Brazil, is designed to develop teaching and research in political science. It has made funds available for advanced training in public administration, with emphasis on research, at the Di Tella Institute. Through the Institute of Public Administration, in New York, the Foundation provides fellowships, consultants, and technical assistance for the Venezuelan Foundation for Community Development and Municipal Improvement. The development of management training for business is the purpose of its grants to the Monterrey Institute of Technology in Mexico and to the Getúlio Vargas Foundation for assistance to the São Paulo School of Business Administration. The Vargas Foundation has also received aid for its research programs in public administration. In Argentina, the Ford Foundation provided funds to the Foundation for Latin American Economic Research for a staff of economists to study industrial problems and trade expansion. It assisted the University of São Paulo in developing its graduate economics center. The development of competence in the area of population and development was encouraged by grants to the Division of Population Studies of the Colombian Association of Faculties of Medicine and the Peruvian Center of Studies on Population and Development.

Latin American Studies in the United States. Since 1962 the Ford Foundation has made a special effort to strengthen Latin American studies in the United States. It has made grants to several universities to support faculty, research, graduate training, and visiting professors from Latin America. The disciplinary emphasis in these programs has been on the social sciences.

The Foundation supports the Social Science Research Council program of providing research opportunities in Latin America for North American faculty members through postdoctoral fellowships. The Foundation also provides financial aid to the Brookings Institution's program of studies of political development in Latin America.

UNITED NATIONS

The United Nations has tended to emphasize the development of broad guidelines and standards, stressing comparative experience, data gathering, and bibliographic activities. These worldwide and regional efforts, coordinated at UN headquarters by the Public Administration Branch of the Department of Economic and Social Affairs and in Latin America by the Economic Commission for Latin America (ECLA), are designed to support regional and country projects.

Public Administration Assistance to Individual Countries. The following services are available:

1) Expert advisers are attached to ministries or departments or serve as directors and instructors in training institutions.

2) Expert services are provided under the United Nations Programme for the Provision of Operational and Executive Personnel (OPEX), in which experts function as civil servants to the host government. OPEX personnel receive the normal salary and benefits for the national post which they occupy plus a supplement provided by the United Nations.

3) United Nations Special Fund Projects include such activities as supporting the establishment of institutes of public administration and various urban development projects. The Advanced School of Public Administration (ESAP) in Colombia is an example of a Special Fund Project.

4) The UN furnishes fellowships to government officials to enable them to undertake advanced studies or to observe administrative systems in other countries.

United Nations assistance to national governments is coordinated by resident representatives of the UN Development Program (UNDP). These officials, who are accredited to one or more countries, are found throughout Latin America and assist in programming the technical assistance of the United Nations and its specialized agencies.

Regional Services in Public Administration. Two regional advisers in public administration are attached to ECLA in Santiago, Chile. The advisers participate in a wide variety of activities; among other things, they work with survey teams to integrate economic development projects and public administration.

Five United Nation experts, including the director, are attached to the Advanced School for Public Administration in Central America (ESAPAC). Since 1953 this school has provided administrative training for officials of the governments of Central America and Panama. The school also supports the member governments in attempts to improve national performance in public administration.

World-wide Services in Public Administration. Substantive support for public administration projects is also provided by the Public Administration Branch at UN headquarters. Headquarters, through a series of conferences and publications, seeks to distil the experiences of many countries in problems common to all. Their publications commonly offer guidelines and alternative methods of dealing with the problem under consideration. The Public Administration Branch is divided into units that deal with local government, organization and methods, and personnel administration. The Fiscal and Financial Branch, another headquarters unit, provides the same type of support in the areas of financial technical assistance and collaborates with the Public Administration Branch.

Latin America has not often been the scene of United Nations public administration conferences, largely because the OAS and IDB have assumed the responsibility of holding such conferences. There is a paucity, therefore, of UN literature directly related to public administration in the countries of Latin America.

THE WORLD BANK

The World Bank engages in public administration activities through its function as a lending institution rather than by means of projects designed to promote administrative competence in general. The fact that the Bank specializes in loans for the provision of foreign exchange rather than local currency places its general emphasis even further from sponsorship of formal training programs in administration. A partial exception is the work of the Economic Development Institute, described below.

Public Administration Activities in Support of Loans. The concern of the Bank with the development of administrative capabilities stems from the widely shared conviction of its officers that administrative competence, or the lack of it, is a critical element in the success or failure of the projects for which the Bank makes loans. Thus, while administrative capacity is an important consideration in the formulation of any loan agreement, loans are not granted for the sole purpose of developing administration.

The Bank traditionally has stressed basic utilities in its lending, with emphasis on the provision of electric power and improvement of transportation facilities. In 1963 it was reported that 90 per cent of Bank activity in the Americas had been for power and transportation. Recently the Bank has been increasingly concerned with agricultural development.

In general the Bank will not finance a project until it is satisfied that the recipient institution has adequate managerial and organizational capabilities. Consultant firms are often engaged, using funds provided through the loan, to assist in situations where administrative capabilities are obviously weak. General organizational restructuring is a fairly common prerequisite to Bank aid. The Bank feels strongly that its projects should be financially viable and as free as possible from political interference. A common tactic involves taking a project or program out of a regular ministry and placing it in an independent public agency. Bank representatives or management consultants assist in these reorganizations.

Technical Assistance Related to Public Administration. The Bank has sent many special missions to conduct broad economic surveys and to study specific economic problems in order to advise governments on the promotion of economic development. Comprehensive surveys have been undertaken in British Guiana, Colombia, Cuba, Guatemala, Jamaica, Mexico, Nicaragua, Panama, Surinam, Venezuela, Argentina, Brazil, and Peru. Although it is uncommon for public administrators to be members of the Bank's survey teams (indeed there is no one in the Bank organization with a title indicating responsibility for administrative considerations), the Bank has given considerable attention to problems of public administration on all government levels.

Resident advisers to governments are stationed from time to time in Latin American republics, and the Bank has an adviser on planning organization who counsels Bank personnel in Washington, Bank resident representatives abroad, and member governments on planning, administration, and organization.

The Economic Development Institute. The Institute was organized in 1955 as an experiment in distilling the Bank's international experiences for the benefit of senior officials of developing countries. The Institute, based in Washington, D.C., has offered numerous courses, conducted in French or Spanish, for these officials, and a number of Latin Americans have participated. Two types of courses are offered: a general development course and courses in functional areas. The general development course deals with generic problems of development. The attention given to planning and programming, fiscal policy, and public finance is of special relevance to public administration.

The courses are geared to an audience described as "on the way up toward policy planning responsibilities." Those in attendance occupy positions roughly equivalent to the U.S. bureau or division chief level, though they are generally younger than would be their U.S. counterparts.

ORGANIZATION OF AMERICAN STATES (OAS)

OAS activities impinging on public administration center in, but are not confined to, the Public Administration Unit of the Department of Economic Affairs. Thus far the major thrust of the public administration unit has been a program designed to gather, analyze, and systemize a variety of data relating to public administration activities in Latin America. The data are organized, by country, into administrative monographs which, in turn, are integrated into a more broadly conceived series of country studies being prepared by the Inter-American Committee on the Alliance for Progress (CIAP). Both the administrative monographs and the country studies provide information relevant to development planning. Illustrative of these studies are ones covering Argentina, Bolivia, Chile, Colombia, Ecuador, Paraguay, Peru, and Venezuela. The monographs, while they seek to be objective rather than prescriptive, do identify certain administrative problems.

Public Administration Conferences. A second major activity of the public administration unit has been the sponsorship of a series of conferences. The first, on organization and methods, held in Rio de Janeiro in 1963, was jointly sponsored by the OAS and the Getúlio Vargas Foundation. The conference report contains the following statement:

> It is generally accepted that most of the basic weaknesses of the administrative machines of Latin American countries stem from the structural inadequacy, their obsolete methods of operation, and their cumbersome procedures. The low rate of productivity found in Latin American Public Administration seems, to a great extent, to be a direct consequence of such structural and operational defects.

A second seminar was held in 1964 in Bogotá on administration of development plans and programs. A third, on development administration, met in Buenos Aires in December, 1965. The basic objective was to study the results and practical gains attributable to the two previous seminars.

OAS-IDB-ECLA Committee on Coordination. Established in 1960 to coordinate the technical assistance efforts of these organizations, the Committee does its work through tripartite missions which advise governments in programming for economic development. Among the countries having received such missions are: Costa Rica, the Dominican Republic, El Salvador, Guatemala, Honduras, Haiti, Nicaragua, Paraguay, Peru, and Uruguay.

OAS-IDB Joint Tax Program. Initially this program was also sponsored by ECLA, but ECLA no longer supports it. Participation in country studies and technical assistance in the field of structural and administrative tax reforms make up the bulk of the program.

The OAS Fellowship Program. On an annual basis, the OAS offers several hundred fellowships to students of the hemisphere in a wide variety of academic fields, including, among others, business administration, architecture and planning, statistics, and law. Undoubtedly a number of the students training under this program find their way into the public service.

The OAS Professorship Program. Under a continuing program of visiting professorships, the OAS has provided opportunities for Latin American scholars to carry out research in such fields as community organization and development, sociology, demography, and urban economics.

THE INTER-AMERICAN DEVELOPMENT BANK (IDB)

In much the same manner as the World Bank, IDB is concerned with the administrative resources available to implement projects connected with its loan activities. IDB, however, participates in a variety of activities, some of which are specifically concerned with a general increase in administrative competence. In all of its technical assistance activities, the IDB aim "is to ensure the most effective use of the funds allocated for investments and to increase the member countries' capacity to absorb external resources."

Direct IDB Support to Institutions. The Bank collaborated with the United Nations Special Fund in the establishment of the Latin American Institute for Economic and Social Planning (ILSPES) in Santiago, Chile. The Institute provides training to government officials in the area of national planning and programming. The IDB share in this venture was approximately $1 million. IDB also provides fellowships for those attending ILAPES.

The Center for Latin American Monetary Studies (CEMLA), a creation of the Central Bank of the Latin American Republics, receives financial support from IDB for four-month courses in Mexico City dealing with the preparation of specific projects and the analysis of financial problems. Since 1962, the Bank has given approximately $500,000 a year for course work and in addition has provided some fellowship aid.

The IDB supports a graduate program in public administration at the Latin American Faculty of Social Sciences (FLACSO) in Santiago, Chile. It also supports the Inter-American School of

Public Administration at the Vargas Foundation in Rio de Janeiro. Through these two efforts the Bank seeks to provide at least basic graduate training in public administration to both Spanish- and Portuguese-speaking Latin Americans.

Other Public Administration Activities. IDB participates with the OAS and ECLA in tripartite advisory committees on national planning and with the OAS in the Joint Tax Program. The Bank also sponsors a series of courses at its Washington headquarters for Latin American officials on the policies and procedures of the Bank and other international finance agencies, as related to project financing.

PRIVATE ORGANIZATIONS

The Rockefeller Foundation. Under its University Development Program, the Foundation is attempting to strengthen political science programs at two universities in Colombia. At both the University of the Valley in Cali and the University of the Andes in Bogotá the Foundation is supporting visiting professors in political science who are developing research and teaching programs in this field.

The Carnegie Corporation of New York. By the terms of its charter, the Carnegie Corporation is limited to the support of scholarship and educational programs within the United States and selected British Commonwealth countries. Its concern with Latin America is expressed through grants to United States scholars and institutions. It has, for example, supported a study of the role of education in political development in Latin America, and it was instrumental in organizing the Committee for the Comparative Study of New Nations (including Latin America) at the University of Chicago.

Council on Higher Education in the American Republics (CHEAR). The basic objective of CHEAR is to promote the exchange of ideas between university leaders in Latin America and their opposites in the United States. Supported jointly by the Carnegie Corporation and the Ford Foundation, CHEAR limits its membership to a small number of educators from the United States and Latin America. Because of a policy of rotating its membership, however, its sphere of influence is constantly being extended.

Resources for the Future (RFF). The objectives of RFF are to advance "the development, conservation, and use of natural resources through programs of research and education." The RFF Latin American program is of recent origin. Of particular relevance is the investigation in which it is participating at the Institute of Social and Economic Planning in Santiago, Chile, centering upon problems arising from the rapid urbanization taking place in Latin America.

Scholarship Program of the French Government. The French government has made a number of study awards and internship opportunities available to Latin Americans. Some of these were for the study of administration.

Loan Program of the Spanish Government. The government of Spain announced in late 1965 a $1 billion aid program for Latin America for the decade ahead. This program is handled on a bilateral basis, and initiative in seeking funds comes from the countries of Latin America. It is not yet possible to judge the implications of these resources for public administration.

III

Fundamental Considerations in
Public Administration Development

A brief definition of public administration was presented in the Introduction. To restate our view, the public administration of a country is the total process of conducting its public services. Thus, it is much more than the effective functioning of an "ideal type" bureaucracy. Public administration is the conduct of government's programs in such fields as agriculture, education, industrial development, health, and transportation. Public administration is the operation of legislative bodies, national, state, and local. It is the functioning of the courts and the systems of law enforcement, the conduct of state and local administrations, and the operation of the nation's political parties.

At the root of a nation's system of public administration are certain fundamental conditions which are deeply influencing and must be understood before changes of a basic nature can be successfully attempted. Since we are concerned with strategies for development, attention needs to be directed to these fundamentals; the alternative would be to propose only moves of surface impact and significance. While we cannot say that our categorization of fundamentals offers the sole appropriate approach, it does try to encompass the most important basic matters. These are taken up as the processes of political socialization, the nature of civic cultures, and the structure and functioning of governments. A fourth element is of a slightly different order. It relates to the character of the knowledge resources that are essential for public administration development; it is discussed as the need for empirically grounded training in the social sciences.

20

THE PROCESSES OF POLITICAL SOCIALIZATION

Some understanding of a nation's public administration can be had by examining its citizenry's outlook toward government and its institutions and programs. This tends to be true irrespective of whether governments are democratic or authoritarian, socialist or free-enterprise oriented, or mixed in their approaches to management of the economy; parliamentary, presidential, or otherwise directed. For example, British subjects take great pride in their government; they feel responsible for its operations as manifested by their keen interest in parties, elections, and in the day-to-day conduct of public affairs. Similar attitudes and behaviors characterize Chile and Costa Rica. In other countries with complex populations and environments, such as Peru, it is more difficult to characterize the outlook of the citizenry.

How citizens feel about their governments, what they expect, what they are willing to contribute, in other words the values which they bring to governmental affairs, can be observed in two major ways. The first is in response to the opportunities that are to be found in any country for citizen participation. Do people go to the polls when they have the opportunity? Do they support their government by paying taxes? Do they communicate their needs and interests to public officials? Do they willingly serve in the various ways, formal and informal, which are often open to the interested citizen, through running for office, through voluntary work on civic projects, advisory bodies, etc.?

The second is in the attitudes toward their work of citizens employed by government. Is a public job a sinecure or a trust or a combination of these? Is public employment a privilege and an obligation (as in Britain, for example) as well as a means of earning a living? Or is it simply an economic base from which one may move on to better opportunities?

Behind the behaviors toward government of each nation's population lies a complex web of conditioning events. It is apparent that a few great historical occurrences have been and remain significant in influencing values and behaviors for Latin America as a whole. The fact that America, from Mexico southward, was a colonial domain, dominated in its intellectual and socio-economic life by the values, purposes, and interests of Spain and Portugal remains today a major force. The fact that Roman Catholicism accompanied the conquistadors and that the Church rapidly gained a permanent place at the emotional center of life is a condition common to most of Latin America. And yet such generalizations as these do not bear with too facile application. The colonialism of Portugal tended to be considerably more benign and pragmatic than that of Spain. This, it is said, in part accounts for the tendency of Brazilians in their governmental affairs, to adapt, accommodate, and compromise. The marked differences which exist between the influence of the Catholic church in Mexico and in Colombia, for example, are further evidence that generalizations for Latin America in its entirety cannot be made too readily.

It is perhaps no easier, though ultimately more productive, to direct attention to the conditioning events which frame citizen values toward governments in individual countries. If one may speculate for illustrative purposes, it is a fascinating riddle to think about the rise of Peronism in Argentina and the forces which brought it about. What part in this phenomenon was played by the admixture of German, Anglo-Saxon, Italian, and Spanish cultures; what part by Argentina's relative geographic remoteness from the centers of Spanish colonial power and, at a later date, from the centers of European industrial development? What have been the effects of its wealth and its relatively hospitable climate and terrain?

When one asks similar questions about Brazil, the task grows more complex. In Brazil ethnic differences and attendant cultural variations, not to mention a vast geography, suggest a citizenry molded quite otherwise than in Argentina. Nonetheless both nations experienced, in overlapping time periods, the rise of popular dictatorships which manifested many similar characteristics. Whether analogous influences were at work in both societies is another intriguing puzzle. The striking differences to be found among Latin American nations are generally acknowledged. For example, Argentina is as different from Brazil as Venezuela is from the United States. There is no homogeneity in the term *Latin America*. Indeed, the term serves to obscure the fundamental variations which are probably best grasped by trying to learn what causes the citizen to think, feel, and act as he does toward his government. These variations must ultimately be appreciated by the scholars and men of affairs in each country as well as by their friends abroad if governments are to be brought to a greater degree of effectiveness.

At least two levels of investigation are needed. The first relates to understanding what transpires in each culture and major subculture with respect to the socialization of the young and in particular the formulation of his political values. The second is concerned with what the individual does with the social and political values he has acquired in childhood, as he functions as citizen, bureaucrat, or civic or political leader.

In the countries of Latin America very little research has been directed either to understanding the nature of the processes which shape the social character of the young; still less to the formative experiences which are ultimately conditioning for political or civic behavior. Indeed, this whole field is an area of investigation as yet hardly touched. It is almost equally true in the United States.

To develop the interest and the research capabilities in each country of Latin America to conduct studies on the processes of political socialization is, of course, a fundamental necessity.

Sociology and economics are as well advanced as any of the social sciences in Latin America, particularly in Chile, Brazil, and Argentina. There are important sociologists in several other countries as well. On the other hand political science as a discipline, and consequently as a field of research, is virtually nonexistent in all of Latin America.[1]

It may be observed parenthetically that not only is research on political socialization lacking, as well as the resources for such research, but were knowledge available there would still be the problem of how it might be used. Essentially the issue is, can

---

[1] An issue of *The Annals* of the American Academy of Political and Social Science (September, 1965) on "Political Socialization: Its Role in the Political Process" indicates the state of research and suggests many of the questions that need to be explored if a better grasp is to be had of the significance of the socializing processes for future political behavior. Probably the most important national study in this field is Lucian W. Pye's book, *Burma: Politics, Personality, and Nation Building* (New Haven: Yale University Press, 1962). No such study exists for any Latin American country.

the young be offered experiences which will produce citizens who are participants in and who are capable of responding to, using, and directing the modernizing processes in their societies?

THE NATURE OF CIVIC CULTURES

The civic attitudes and behaviors of the adult are in need of a wide variety of investigation. What does the citizen expect of his governments? What kinds of responsibilities does he feel toward these governments? What are his views on the ballot? How does he feel about the Church as a political force? Does he have special perceptions with regard to the role of the military? What are the evidences of a sense of national purpose, of a common sharing of goals with other citizens? To what degree are various segments of the population so engrossed in their tasks of survival that little or no attention goes into civic interests and activities? What attitudes exist toward bureaucrats as a class or toward selected elements of the bureaucracy like the police or tax collectors? What civic values—or lack of them—are found in the bureaucracy? How are politicians appraised and what is perceived as the role of political parties? What, in particular, are the civic values of leadership groups, potential and actual: students, labor leaders, churchmen, business managers and entrepreneurs, landholders and working farmers above the subsistence level, politicians, senior bureaucrats?

Knowledge of the civic values and interests which prevail in any given country is an essential ingredient for political leaders who are concerned with modernization. To the extent that citizens are interested and confident in their government, they are likely to participate in the tasks of national development. On the other hand, if citizens view government as distant, hostile, irresponsible and biased, the political leader's work of mobilizing for the modernization of his nation will be infinitely more difficult. He should know what his resources and his chances are.

Obviously, to obtain a clear perception of a nation's civic culture, or rather civic cultures, is an enormously complex task. To modify these cultures is a long, slow, process, extending over generations.

Political and other leaders usually have an awareness, sometimes keen, sometimes dim, of the civic values which animate the various segments of their nation. Such perceptions come through response at the ballot box, student riots, land seizures, and labor agitation; the responsiveness of citizens to meeting their tax obligations; the quality of personnel seeking employment or actually employed in government; the newspapers, radio, television, and other forms of communication, formal and casual. But more often than not the understanding which the politician has of these matters is more visceral than precise.

The task at hand can be met only if the leadership in each country is persuaded of its necessity. For it is quite apparent that developing an understanding of citizen attitudes cannot be the work of outsiders primarily. The subjects are too delicate; the need for inherent sensitivity to the country situation too great to permit a substantial role for the foreign investigator.

A number of modest but encouraging efforts are moving forward in various countries in Latin America. Several of these take their inspiration from the work of Professors Gabriel Almond and Sidney Verba, who in their volume *The Civic Culture*[2] studied basic political attitudes in Mexico, Germany, Italy, Great Britain, and the United States. By conducting detailed interviews with thousands of persons, they were able to formulate profiles of the civic values which seem to characterize, in strikingly different ways, the several countries. While some of their assumptions and techniques have been questioned, and are now undergoing evaluation and refinement, the significance of this pioneering effort remains very great.

Almond and Verba's work has been influential in leading a group of young political sociologists in Brazil to begin exploring civic values in the state of Minas Gerais. Their work was undoubtedly of importance in the formulation of a research program presently under way at CENDES, the Center for Studies of Development at the Universidad Central de Venezuela, in cooperation with the Massachusetts Institute of Technology. The first of the published data from this program, which is concerned with conflict and consensus among labor leaders, explores labor atti-

[2] (Princeton, N.J.: Princeton University Press, 1963).

tudes about politics, the nation, state and city governments, education, economic issues, and a number of other matters. The Almond and Verba work has also been influential in the development of the research program at the Centro Latino Americano de Colombia (CLAMCO) in the University of the Andes, Bogotá, which seeks to develop an understanding of noneconomic factors of significance for development through exploring political values, and party and economic activities of national, state, and local party leaders.

In Guatemala a series of studies of the national social structure, sponsored by the Guatemalan National Council for Economic Planning, is under way, with emphasis on the national power structure as it relates to the rural areas of the country. The fieldwork, conducted largely by young Guatemalan scholars, is carried on under the general leadership of the Institute of Latin American Studies of the University of Texas.

Several points can be noted from this experience. First, the research has been or is being conducted largely by nationals within each country. It is true that North American research guidance and leadership is being used, but there is recognition that "civic culture" studies must be indigenously handled and must have responsible backing from significant elements of the national leadership. Second, these studies have tended to concentrate on leadership groups, e.g., labor leaders and political party leaders, as a means of entering the field at vital points. Such an approach is essential since it provides a means of delimiting and reducing to manageable scope what otherwise is an overwhelmingly large and amorphous task. Third, the financing of these efforts has come primarily from foreign sources thus far. It seems clear that external assistance cannot be the source of support indefinitely, and that if substantial continuing efforts are to be made they must primarily be financed from within. Indeed, given the sensitive nature of this field of inquiry, support from internal sources is much to be preferred. Finally with this recitation of "civic culture" type studies one comes close to exhausting the evidence of such work presently under way.

This is not surprising. The number of Latin American scholars capable of conducting fieldwork in the social sciences is extremely limited. A few other institutions exist, beyond those mentioned, which do, or presumably could, carry on such research including, for example, the Monterrey (Mexico) Institute of Technology, the Latin American Faculty of Social Sciences (FLACSO), in Santiago, the Di Tella Institute in Buenos Aires, the Getúlio Vargas Foundation in Rio de Janeiro, and the Faculty of Philosophy at São Paulo. As we note subsequently, one of the very great needs in Latin America is to build teaching and research competence in the social sciences.

THE STRUCTURE AND FUNCTIONING OF GOVERNMENTS

Writing in 1964 about research on government and politics in Latin America, Professor Merle Kling observed:

> Certain omissions in the literature dealing with Latin American political life verge on the scandalous. There are no book-length studies by political scientists of Brazil since Vargas or of Argentina since Perón. There is no book-length study of Chilean politics since World War II. Despite the dramatic emergence of a professedly Marxist-Leninist government in Cuba, there is no book-length study by a political scientist of contemporary Cuban politics.[3]

The comment was primarily addressed to political scientists of the United States. Since, however, the discipline of political science is virtually nonexistent in Latin America, few resources exist there for filling the gaps.

Perhaps in no other field than government and politics is the paucity of factual and analytical information so striking. In some countries it is virtually impossible to obtain an accurate picture of the formal structure of the national government. Such matters as the size and composition of the bureaucracy, the numbers, nature, and functions of independent or quasi-independent government corporations, the scope of operations of state, departmental, and local governments, the actual processes of governmental control over public expenditures, and the organization and operation of legislatures, political parties, courts, and law enforcement

[3] Charles Wagley (ed.), *Social Science Research in Latin America* (New York: Columbia University Press, 1964), 196.

agencies are largely unrecorded and unanalyzed. Simple structural and factual data (not to mention data derived from an examination of actual functions or operations) are so lacking as to make teaching about government and politics quite difficult. In many countries, either for teaching purposes or to permit work on or in governmental institutions, it is necessary first to engage in rudimentary fact gathering. This situation, little appreciated either within or outside of Latin America, is significant in connection with the whole drive toward modernization.

Without the means to understand how legislatures function, how presidents conduct their offices, how ministries are organized and operate, how bureaucrats are selected and how they perform, and how urban areas are changing, for example, the essential knowledge is lacking which will permit experimentation and development of the instruments of government. And these, of course, are the basic tools for modernization. Governments incapable of sustaining themselves, providing essential legislation, amassing the resources needed for development programs, and managing the economy in such vital respects as controlling inflation and maintaining adequate foreign exchange will contribute to stagnation rather than to modernization.

A good many observers of the Latin American governmental scene are prone to make continental or even global generalizations, which at times do have a certain utility. One astute North American, for example, has commented on the youthfulness of Latin American bureaucrats and upon the necessity, in their less functionalized and specialized societies, of their playing numerous roles, technical, advisory, and political. This suggests a somewhat different kind of proposition for public service than is customary in the United States.

A comment by Professor Frank Brandenberg is also in the vein of the useful broad generalization. He has written that:

> The president who comes to office in Latin America has none of the assurance and strength provided by a political party that has deep roots in the thousands of communities that form the nation. That is why he has to be the architect of his own power. He has no institutional backing except the army, and the army is unpredictable. It may support the

president one day and turn him out the next. That is why he has to surround himself with people "de absoluta confianza."[4]

But essentially the development of knowledge about governments and the political process must be generated on an individual country basis. Again the task is very great. However, the use of external assistance may be more feasible than in the case of studies of political socialization and of civic values. For one thing, a great deal of the preliminary need is for simple data gathering. For another, Latin America is attuned to having foreign assistance for purposes of speeding socio-economic development, and governmental leaders are increasingly aware of the need for skilled help in dealing with their governmental inadequacies. There is responsiveness to tax teams and planning advisory teams made up, in part, of foreign experts. What is needed, beyond readiness to deal with specific governmental administrative and political problems, sometimes with outside help, is to recognize that a major analytical effort lasting for a considerable period (and in some modified form continuing permanently) is essential if government and politics in their many ramifications are first to be understood, and then made to work, with greater effectiveness.

THE NEED FOR EMPIRICALLY GROUNDED TRAINING IN THE SOCIAL SCIENCES

The intellectual traditions which dominate the universities in all of Latin America, with almost no exceptions, are European. Much emphasis is placed on the development of an understanding of historical and philosophical perspectives. The student is exposed to considerable theorizing about systems and to generalization and abstraction. Considerably greater attention seems to be given to matters having metaphysical content than to the development of observational skills and empirical evidence. This is far less the case in the natural sciences.

Faculties of law produce the largest number of students ulti-

---

[4] Frank Tannenbaum (ed.), *Ten Keys to Latin America* (New York: Random House, 1959), 159.

mately occupying prominent positions in public affairs. The programs of instruction are dominated by European civil law and the deductive approaches which have characterized legal scholarship in civil law countries. Conventional practice is to "annotate the masters." As Kenneth L. Karst has observed:

> Much of the Latin American [legal] literature is barren. It naturally is representative of the current style of legal analysis. There is article after article on the true nature of one concept or another, including polemics carried on for years without any of the participants going beyond logical deductions from the codes or from the writings of the great jurists. . . . The articles written by students which usually win prizes in competitions are generally of the classical type. They show the most "scholarship," i.e., familiarity with the classics. Originality is sometimes rewarded, but it is a stylized and conceptual kind of originality, the ability to make new deductions from old sources.[5]

The situation in the law faculties is changing very slowly. Under the impact of widespread development activities it is coming to be recognized that those trained in the law are poorly prepared to deal with the legal aspects of modernization—with agrarian and tax reform, industrial development, issues of urbanization, etc. As of the moment the law faculties that have shown a serious concern with relating the teaching of law to problems of development are in Chile, Costa Rica, and Brazil. In addition, a few institutions outside of the law faculties of universities, such as the Vargas Foundation in Brazil, offer courses for practicing lawyers to encourage a better grasp of the legal aspects of development.

Political science, as previously noted, is a virtually unknown discipline in Latin American universities. The situation with political science reveals part of the central difficulty in the development of young intellectuals capable of undertaking tasks of modernization in Latin America. For the universities, dominated as they in good measure are, by students more interested in political ideology than in the serious study of society as it exists, do not provide an environment for empirically grounded learning. Some

[5] Wagley, *Social Science Research*, 295.

few exceptions are to be found; for example, the engineering and agricultural universities in Lima, the University of Chile and the Catholic University in Santiago, the University of Costa Rica in San José, the University of the Andes in Bogotá, and the University of the Valley in Cali, Colombia. But even in these institutions the development of political science as a discipline is, at best, in a rudimentary stage.

Carlos Masad, the Chilean economist, has observed, "Most Latin American economists prefer to set up hypotheses and present them in a polemical way rather than test them against data."[6] While this is in the expected tradition, nonetheless the field of economics has tended to prosper under the impact of the continental drive toward socio-economic development. The Alliance for Progress requirement that each nation prepare a development plan has forced serious attention to at least macroeconomic indicators. The expectations of the various international lending agencies have caused governments to prepare detailed economic justifications for their project proposals and to begin to come to terms with their continuing needs for well-grounded data and capable economic analysts. A number of universities, perhaps most notably those in Chile, are making good progress in reordering their curricula in the field of economics and in relating the discipline to problems of modernization.

Sociology, possibly because it is the "science" of society and therefore has appeal to the intellectual's taste for speculation about the nature of man, society, and the state, has had a relatively encouraging development in recent years. Growth in the discipline is evident in Rio de Janeiro and São Paulo, in Santiago at FLACSO, in Colombia, Venezuela, and in a few other places. Nonetheless, as Professor Rex Hopper has observed:

> Teaching is speculative, content eclectic, subject matter poorly defined, teachers are largely untrained and unspecialized, little research is undertaken, and what there is continues the tradition of the "pensadores," for very few investigators have been trained in modern methods of research.[7]

6 *Ibid.,* 223.
7 *Ibid.,* 255.

With the exceptions noted earlier, there is only the most limited capability for the conduct of studies, essentially sociological in nature, into political socialization and the nature of civic cultures.

Important anthropological work has been carried on in Latin America. Much of this has centered on the Indian, and almost all of the significant research has been undertaken by North Americans. It is typical of anthropological research that it tends to be more absorbed with ancient and traditional cultures than with cultural issues of immediate relevance to the contemporary scene. Relatively little attention has been given by anthropologists to the striking phenomenon of urbanization which is sweeping the Southern Hemisphere. Most of the trained anthropologists in the universities have been educated abroad, primarily in the United States.

Geography, such a significant subject to the understanding of cultural and political development in Latin America, is found primarily in Brazilian universities and at the University of Chile. The Geographical Institute of the University of Chile devotes itself to research in a wide range of sub-fields such as physical geography, regional geography, and planning. But as in other fields in the social sciences much of the work of Latin American geographers is historical in character. Largely ignored have been such important current problems as urbanization and population growth.

The rise of the social sciences in the United States has followed different intellectual traditions. The common law, with its emphasis on interpretation and consequently on adaptation, has been one important influence. The Protestant ethic, with its consequences for the growth of pragmatism and empiricism, is clearly another. Perhaps of greater significance to any discussion concerned with Latin America is that the sciences, physical and social, were seen from the earliest days of the American Republic as aids of government. Thus a highly pragmatic aura surrounded much scientific research. From their inception, the universities, especially the great state institutions of the Middle and Far West, took on the role of being the scientific research arms of their state governments. For a nation that was settling its frontier lands and going through the experience of rapid modernization, this was an invaluable asset. To have the universities thus view themselves, and to have physical and social scientists alike devoting their talents to solving the practical problems encountered by industry, agriculture, and government, gave great impetus to development. Not all of the consequences were beneficial, of course. Until very recently the largely applied character of American science has meant that much fundamental knowledge had to be drawn from western European sources. The often-observed lack of cultural and historical depth in American society was another unfelicitous result. Nonetheless a strong empirical social science research tradition is now a part of the North American academic environment. It is probable that one of the most profoundly important contributions which can be made to development in Latin America will be to assist in communicating the relevant aspects of U.S. experience with the growth of the social sciences.

This short discussion of fundamental considerations scarcely communicates sympathetic awareness of the profound and difficult tasks which are implied. Those concerned with aiding the processes of modernization are often damned for superficiality; they infrequently have concerned themselves with the basic and long-term tasks. Striking a balance between measures to deal with root problems and those which will yield evidence of current progress is a game played differently according to one's disposition and position. It seems certain on the evidence, however, that most of the ideas with regard to public administration development have not focused on fundamentals. Beyond those fundamentals are a host of operational considerations which further compound the effort. We discuss some of these in Chapter IV.

IV

Some Operational Considerations

Having discussed some of the more fundamental conditions and needs which must be addressed if public administration development is to occur in Latin America, we turn now to another level of consideration. In the current, continuing work of modernization, observers and participants can detect a variety of factors, some limiting, some encouraging, some of unspecified consequence, which have not too frequently been called to attention with specific reference to public administration development. The common element among these factors is their relatively direct impact on current activities. Thus we call them operational considerations; they include the pressures for rapid development, the requirement for political support, country "style," donor "style," communication and coordination, and institutional competence. While making no case for their completeness, we believe that they represent several of the more important matters which need to be reflected on and dealt with by those concerned with public administration development.

THE PRESSURES FOR RAPID DEVELOPMENT

All of the parties engaged in the modernization of Latin America are aware of the profound human deprivations which are everywhere evident. It is not necessary to dwell on the facts of illiteracy, disease, unemployment and underemployment, and inadequate housing, clothing, and food, which makes life for millions of Latin Americans a grim struggle. The larger costs, in terms of lost creativity and submerged intelligence, are ones that can hardly be thought about in the face of so much simple physical necessity.

These conditions are the primary concern of virtually all of

34

the governments of Latin America. They deal with their problems in ways that vary according to national circumstance. In Brazil, for example, a persistent issue is control of inflation and inauguration of financial policies which will assure the availability of foreign credit and currencies. In Chile, along with a vigorous program of social development, considerable attention is being given to improving agricultural production in order to reduce the drain on foreign reserves caused by food purchases abroad. But at the same time they are pursuing such "main line" policies, these governments, and most others, are pressing and being pressed to take measures which will reach and better the lives of the individual citizen.

Indeed, the capacity of governments to survive depends to a considerable degree on the results they can produce for the citizenry. While substantial numbers of Latin Americans are still politically inert, most observers believe that the levels of unrest are rising throughout the whole of the continent and that the only alternatives are modernization or social explosion. Thus the pressures are largely in the direction of dealing with the present, and of deferring both thought and resources with respect to more basic cultural and institutional changes.

Institutions concerned with modernization are expected to produce immediate evidences of success. The Alliance for Progress was conceived as a ten-year program, and since the end of the first year responsible Washington officials have been asking "to see results." International agencies engaged in development activities in Latin America wish to justify their efforts to their national members by revealing specific accomplishments, and the private foundations also live under some impetus to show "results." Thus for understandable reasons short-run objectives tend to take precedence over moves of a long-term fundamental character.

The impact of this situation on public administration development is found in many quarters. While governments realize that they lack the administrative and technical skills to organize and operate their social, economic, and physical development programs, they find it difficult either to allocate more than token resources to education and training for the public service or to release their few able personnel for training at home or abroad. Much of the United States assistance in public administration under the Alliance for Progress has been for "spot jobs," for example, tax, customs, budget, and accounting reform. Some U.S. help has gone into the development of schools or institutes of public administration, but usually with expectations of substantial quantitative results (numbers of technicians trained) within a very short time period. The United Nations has contributed its share of personnel to specific limited technical assistance tasks. Perhaps only the Ford Foundation, with its interest in encouraging the growth of social science capabilities in selected universities, has inclined toward a longer range view of what may be needed.

The pressure for results has the great merit that it frequently forces realism into development efforts. It has the psychological benefit of helping to overcome normal inertias. But it tends also to displace concern for fundamental issues with regard to public administration development.

THE REQUIREMENT FOR POLITICAL SUPPORT

Experience has shown that public administration projects, programs, and training institutions must have strong, high-level political support to be successful. The reasons are fairly apparent. Any action program of significance will be certain to affect established and influential interests. For example, moves to make public employment subject to standards of selection will interfere with patronage and nepotism, usually the prerogatives of the party in power. Improvements in tax administration, in countries where there is widespread evasion, can be a serious challenge to the regime and to those instituting the improvements. Even such endeavors as research on problems of the public service or training programs for governmental personnel may be viewed as sufficiently threatening to generate strong negative responses from powerful segments of the community.

Modifications in other institutions of a nation's public administration—the legislative bodies, the courts, and the political parties—are fraught with hazards; they demand from the political leadership the greatest judgment, courage, and tactical skill. Even a relatively simple proposal, concerning improvement of the technical and library resources available to the Congress, was a matter of controversy in Peru. The more far-reaching effort of President Branco in Brazil to force a semblance of coherence into the country's political party structure required extraordinary political determination.

Improving the public administration of a nation has little immediate citizen appeal. True, in the long run programs of great importance such as land reform, the elimination of slums and the development of clinical health programs, which operate successfully because of competent organization and administration, may bring great credit to a government. Typically, however, relatively few pressures arise from the citizenry for improved governmental operations. The lack of internal pressure for administrative improvement, the lack of clear benefits to be gained in the short run, and the costs in terms of probable opposition that must be absorbed—all these are deterrents to positive high-level response.

It thus becomes unusually important for political leaders to have an appreciation of the significance, to social and economic development, of governmental competence and of the varied ways in which this must be sought. Beyond providing the necessary backing themselves, they must ordinarily also develop, in their closest political colleagues and in the larger leadership of the country, an awareness of the need. The most far-sighted political leader may want to go a further step and encourage awareness of the problems and needs of modern governmental administration in the emerging generation of political leaders.

THE COUNTRY "STYLE"

To the leadership of Latin America the distinctive character of each nation is an accepted condition. Partly because of the language factor and partly for historical reasons the great variations from country to country are far less apparent to outsiders. What we have chosen to call the "style" of a country is, of course the composite of geography, history, ethnic make-up, and resources. Ultimately a country's style will shape its government—its public administration—and any fundamental effort directed to development in this field must grow out of and build on its style,

Of special significance is the character of a nation's relationships with the outside world and especially with the United States. So much of the external impetus for development comes from the United States that this element of the national style looms large. Every Latin nation has been deeply influenced by the American Constitution and to a lesser degree by U.S. governmental practice. Most technical assistance in public administration draws on U.S. experience; most foreign advisers in Latin America come from the United States.

Two of the operational considerations growing out of differing styles are, then, first the set of unique elements that are strategically important in creating a given style, and secondly the aspect of the style which is influenced by and affects relationships with the United States.

At the risk of great superficiality, but to illustrate the concept of style, we suggest some facets of its appearance. Mexico's development has been significantly affected by its revolution of half a century past and by its proximity to the United States. The revolution set a tone of expectation with regard to social and economic development which has found its way into much progressive legislation over the decades. The fact of virtually one-party government, a derivative of the revolution, with a relative lack of internal competition, has meant that the governmental administration is hardly innovative or particularly efficient. The Mexican experience with the United States has ranged all the way from conflict to close cooperation. In general the Mexican style is to meet the United States in a manner of confident defensiveness with the clear intention of protecting its social gains, resisting interference in its governmental affairs, and taking advantage of American resources and skills as they may be available.

Peru is sometimes looked on as the country having characteristics which are "typically Latin American." Its geography creates a sharp demarcation between coastal cities and the Andean and jungle hinterland. Its indigenous population is remote from the modern life of the coastal towns. Lima was the center of the Spanish colonial empire and still retains the aura of a noble colonial city; it resembles Madrid in its culture, elegance, and social stratification. But Peru is also a country that more than many others is in the throes of transition. Lima is pre-eminent on the western coast of South America as the center of commerce and industry. Its conservative tradition is attractive to foreign investors; no currency in Latin America has been more stable than the Peruvian. And in part because this tradition has tended also to be responsible, governments in Peru, even when they are the products of military coups, tend to be moderately responsive to popular pressures. The Peruvian style, while colonial and elitist, is also intelligently conservative, responsive, and evolutionary. Its external relationships, especially with the United States, tend to reflect this style.

Venezuela, in contrast to Peru, held little attraction for colonial Spain. Until the discovery of oil it was first a colonial and then an independent backwater. In consequence it has no particular aristocracy of lineage; ethnically it is a composite of many influences, Indian, Spanish, African, and North American. Since World War II it has had a considerable influx of other Europeans. The Venezuelan style is almost the frontier style—pragmatic, experimental, volatile, and relatively unmodulated. Signs of pragmatism are found in the considerable attention given by the two most recent governments to the matter of orderly political succession and to the need for economic diversification. Venezuela's external relationships are so extensive and so important that it is probably the most commercially cosmopolitan nation in South America. It views its associations with the United States as essential; it treats them, on the whole, with practical deference.

The different characteristics of each country's style make necessary the most astute assessment and response on the part of participants in Latin American development efforts. But learning national style comes perhaps less from intensive analytical work than from the accumulated experience of many years in association with a given people, culture, and government.

THE DONOR "STYLE"

Our interest here is in briefly characterizing the modes of operation of those organizations—the USAID, the foundations, the international agencies—which are the principal sources of support for training, research, and technical assistance in public administration. Their role at this stage in Latin America's modernization efforts tends to be more that of donor than of participant, and this is bound to affect their operations. They supply funds, technical experts, and training opportunities in the spirit of Point Four. The partnership ideal of the Alliance for Progress is as yet more a hope than a reality in this field, although there are exceptions.

AID, which has missions in all Latin American countries at present, works with country program plans and gives attention to administrative weaknesses that must be overcome if the plans are to be realized. However, it limits its efforts to dealing with administrative deficiencies where the host government is prepared to act. Since a great many administrative problems are related to the development of functional fields such as agriculture, housing, and education, there is a dispersion of responsibility in AID with regard to issues of public administration.

For a variety of reasons the unit within AID in Washington specifically concerned with public administration development— or as it is called, development administration, i.e., administration related to socio-economic development—is severely limited in the perspectives it is able to provide. It is shorthanded, pressed by country missions to recruit contractors or direct-hire technicians, and plagued by burdensome procedural requirements. In consequence the function of stimulating AID country missions to think and act in depth with regard to public administration development, and thus, indirectly, to encourage similar thought and action on the part of Latin American colleagues, is very largely neglected. Virtually no attention is directed to the development of U.S. institutional resources to participate in the public administration effort.

AID country missions, with some exceptions, do not have well-thought-through public administration development programs. Generally speaking, the diagnoses of administrative weaknesses which accompany individual country program analyses reflect a narrow concept of public administration. An exception is AID's development plan for public administration in Guatemala. A similarly well-developed scheme is apparently in the making at present for Brazil.

An added deterrent to breadth and depth of approach results from the AID practice of rotating its field personnel every two years, although there are exceptions. A man just beginning to grasp the range of elements and problems which influence the public administration of a particular country may find himself moved elsewhere. A similar problem exists in the AID tendency to think of contractual arrangements in terms of three to five years, when most public administration development programs need at least ten to fifteen years.

One reason that AID is limited in its ability to operate in sensitive areas such as congressional or party reform is that as an instrument of the U.S. government, its motives may be suspect. The Agency does, of course, have the responsibility of furthering American interests, but the degree to which this influences AID practices is sometimes exaggerated in the eyes of Latin Americans. Such moves as linking AID support to the settlement of oil disputes with U.S. firms, however, has not encouraged accurate perspectives on the Agency's intentions.

The private foundations of the United States—the Ford Foundation, the Rockefeller Foundation, and to a much lesser degree, the Carnegie Corporation of New York—have their own institutional approaches and goals. The Carnegie Corporation, for example, is limited by charter to spending its main fund for the benefit of American institutions and scholars. The Rockefeller Foundation has emphasized scientific and technical work in its Latin American activities.

The Ford Foundation's interest, somewhat in contrast to AID's, lies more in stressing the development of educational facilities and programs which will contribute to long-term growth of competence in public affairs than in meeting immediate technical administrative problems.

The UN, which makes assistance available, upon country request, as an international agency has a bureaucracy with administrators and technicians drawn from member countries. Thus the experience and formal preparation of its technical staff vary greatly. While the prestige of the UN is extraordinarily high, the reaction to its staff in countries receiving technical advice is mixed. Not only are there different levels of competency, but differences of approach inevitably emerge. The necessity for the UN to provide aid to all its members has encouraged reliance on general doctrine and formula approaches to public administration.

The creation of regional training programs has been encouraged by the United Nations, the Inter-American Development Bank, and the Organization of American States. The idea of regional training has obvious appeal to such organizations, and programs have proliferated recently. These programs have of necessity tended to be abstract and general, and students frequently have been unable to gain practical information applicable to their home environment. One promising modification of the regional approach is found in the United Nations' ESAPAC, the regional school in Central America, which is now beginning to offer courses in each of the six Central American countries as a means of providing content that is oriented to the individual countries.

COMMUNICATIONS AND COORDINATION

As an overview is taken of public administration activities in Latin America, it becomes evident that there is less than adequate communication about current efforts among those who are most directly involved. Sufficient coordination between existing and proposed public administration training programs also is lacking. It is apparent that schemes are being launched, especially by international agencies, with inadequate regard to existing training programs and the very limited supply of available talent.

This assessment was indirectly substantiated by the participants in the OAS-supported public administration conference in Buenos Aires in 1965. The directors and other representatives of Latin American schools and institutes of public administration in Latin America informally concluded that the most useful product of the conference was the opportunity it provided to learn about the ongoing organizations and programs in this field. Several participants observed that individual country programs tend to operate in isolation and acknowledged their own lack of awareness of the problems, successes, and failures being encountered elsewhere.

One evidence of this lack of communication is the chaotic situation which exists in connection with program staffing. The limited number of qualified public administration specialists are constantly being approached by the new organizations coming into being. One UN official who is already responsible for an important school indicated that he has been approached about leaving his present position at least five times during the preceding two years. To illustrate the shortage of personnel, the director of one country's institute of administration, though he had ample funds, was simply unable to locate personnel to staff his organization. Chilean government officials, UN personnel, and faculty members of the University of Chile have viewed with concern the BID-supported FLACSO public administration program as a possible duplication of the program already under way at the University of Chile.

A multiplication of endeavors has occurred, with supporting agencies apparently uninformed about, or not particularly concerned with, the goals of existing programs. Overlapping and consequent inefficiency has been the result. In Santiago, which already had two public administration activities, the UN appointed a new adviser to develop public administration activities at its ECLA school. In Rio de Janeiro the EBAP is conducting a vigorous Training and Research program within the Vargas Foundation; BID is supporting its Inter-American School of Public Administration within the same foundation.

Communications are also inadequate with respect to teaching materials, library resources, and current research efforts. While the problem is most accentuated among the individual countries, Brazil has the additional difficulty of poor communications among its own twenty or more public administration training programs. The research conducted in EBAP in Rio de Janeiro and ONRAP in Peru is producing reports and studies which may be of general interest to those engaged in public administration training. An expert who has traveled widely in Latin America looking at public administration libraries finds that the strengths and limitations of individual collections are not understood and that little is known about the adequacy of library resources from institution to institution.

Current experience, if it were better communicated, could be instructive with regard to certain outstandingly successful programs as well as unsuccessful ones. The Venezuelan Foundation for Community Development and Municipal Improvement (COMUN) has made remarkable progress in strengthening the capacities of local governments through a combination of financial, training, and technical assistance efforts. The development of local government competence is a major concern in virtually every country, and the Venezuelan experience can be useful. This is true also of the excellent program of the Brazilian Institute of Municipal Administration. Such a scheme as that developed by the National Institute of Development Administration (INAD) in Guatemala for attracting able university students into public service training programs is imaginative and deserves to be better known. Of the less successful public administration efforts, it might be useful to know more about the problems encountered. Were these programs poorly planned, inadequately financed, lacking in direction and in staff resources? Were they in need of assistance from an external organization, or was such assistance a disability? What are the pitfalls indicated by these experiences?

Some of the more difficult and delicate aspects of public administration development might be encouraged through improved communications. For example, were an analysis of the administrative deficiencies in congressional operations in a given country made and disseminated, it might lead to such analyses being undertaken elsewhere. Knowledge of similar studies of the functioning of political parties, the courts, or law enforcement agencies could have a like effect.

There is a modest but growing interest in the reform of law schools in Latin America to make them more responsive to the legal aspects of development. A few institutions, particularly in Chile, Brazil, and Central America, are in the forefront of this movement. Their efforts should certainly be known. Important events such as the rise of the Central American Common Market and the moves toward a Latin American Common Market call for study of the legal inhibitions to the operation of the markets. A start has been made in Central America through the inauguration of a program of law publications and legal studies under the leadership of the AID Regional Office for Central America and Panama. This enterprise may provide valuable suggestions for the rest of Latin America.

INSTITUTIONAL COMPETENCE

The state of the social sciences in the universities of Latin America has already been reviewed briefly. If capabilities are to be developed for research into social, political, and governmental processes, major administrative changes will have to occur in the universities. Unless the institutions of higher education can move toward control of their internal affairs by professional academicians and boards of public-spirited citizens, and away from domination by politically motivated student and faculty groups, intellectual quality is bound to suffer. The scholar driven, by student agitation, from his university because of foreign support received for badly needed social science research is illustrative of the intellectual consequence of university control by politically inspired interests.

As for the schools and institutes of public administration, they are, generally speaking, very modest in terms of financial resources, physical facilities, depth and quality of staff, breadth and variety of curricula, and output of research. Since for the most part they are quite new and are forced by necessity to concentrate on technician-type subject matter, their limitations are understandable. While all have aspirations to offer broader education programs, few have been able to do so. Research has been largely limited to data gathering for technical assistance projects and teaching.

Most of these institutes exist independently of the universities, principally because affiliation would mean involvement in university political and administrative problems. Except for this, it is probable that university association would by preferred by the directors of many institutes. In any event, the forward-looking leaders of some of the public administration institutes recognize that they must develop working relationships with universities both to strengthen their own teaching and research programs (through cooperative course offerings, exchanges of faculty, and joint research projects) and to encourage university involvement in the processes of educating for public service.

Long-term cooperation between universities in the United States and in Latin America is one of the likeliest routes to strengthening the social sciences and hence public administration training in Latin America. What is the level of competence in Latin American affairs among U.S. institutions? How well prepared are U.S. universities and research institutes to work cooperatively with universities in Latin America?[1]

In 1962 and 1963, at the request of the Ford Foundation, Pro-

[1] Our previous discussions, where they have dealt with non-Latin American institutions, have been concerned with indicating the programs and

fessor Carl Spaeth made an assessment of Latin American studies in the United States. He summarized his observations, in part, as follows:

> ... There are very few highly qualified teachers and scholars in most of the disciplines and many mediocre people with tenure; lack of fundamental data based on recent research that is essential to consideration of contemporary problems; failure by individual scholars, institutions, and the profession as a whole to identify the crucial problems and the questions to be asked; dissipation of resources through duplication by individuals and institutions of unrelated efforts on the same problems and often the same geographic areas; teaching materials, badly outdated both in substance and form, which adhere rigidly and without discrimination to traditional text "coverage" with little or no effort to bring knowledge of the past to bear on problems of today; until very recently, little or no interest among the better college graduates in pursuing Latin American studies; and most seriously, a lack of institutional and national delineation of a rationale for Latin American studies that takes into account the overall needs of and demands upon American higher education.[2]

While Spaeth found a discouraging situation with respect to teaching and research on Latin America, he was not, of course, casting doubt on the quality of teaching and research in general. While there may be very few political scientists, economists, sociologists, historians, and geographers of note who are Latin Americanists, there are numbers of imaginative, innovative scholars in these fields and others whose work has great potentiality for Latin America.

"styles" of external organizations assisting in public administration development. Occasional reference has also been made to U.S. institutions working on public administration and public affairs problems in Latin America. By way of summary, the principal such U.S. organizations are the Brookings Institution, Harvard University, the University of Pittsburgh, the Institute of Public Administration (N.Y.), the Governmental Affairs Institute, and the University of Southern California. In addition, a number of management consulting firms like Collett and Clapp (Puerto Rico) and McKinsey and Company engage in administrative studies and the conduct of training programs.

[2] Unpublished report to the Ford Foundation (March, 1963).

In the years since Spaeth wrote, at least two encouraging developments have occurred. One is the increasing interest in Latin America among U.S. educators. In part this derives from reaffirmation by the U.S. government of its commitment to the Alliance for Progress and the growing appreciation in government circles that U.S. universities must play a very important part in Latin American development. The President, in his message of early February, 1966, acknowledged the urgent need for the federal government to assist American educational institutions in their international endeavors, saying "Over the past two decades, our universities have been a major resource in carrying on development programs around the world. We have made heavy demands upon them. But we have not supported them adequately." Undoubtedly, the effect of this statement eventually will be significant for Latin American studies.

The other development, which followed in part from the Spaeth evaluation, is that substantial foundation grants have been made to about a dozen American universities to build competence in teaching and research related to Latin America. Since, however, to produce the well-trained and seasoned scholar or practitioner is time consuming and costly, we are unlikely to see rapid change in the Latin American capabilities of American universities.

One of the results of unfamiliarity with Latin America is that research and training programs introduced there by American scholars may be impractical. A graduate program in economics, offered in a situation which actually called for the development of undergraduate courses, has been judged a failure by its AID sponsors or, at best, "premature." In public administration, lack of knowledge of the indigenous situation has led to emphasis on form and procedure rather than substance, often with abortive results. If there is to be real growth of expertise in American universities, sustained concentration on individual countries or limited regions will be required. Only thus can knowledge in depth be achieved.

The U.S. government is increasingly turning to universities to assist in training and technical assistance work in Latin America. AID officials are exploring means of overcoming some of the problems inherent in present arrangements. The burden on the individual institution, when it assumes responsibility for a major overseas program, is very heavy. It is not always clear under current practices that one of the residuals will be strengthening resources and capabilities within the U.S. university. Latin American institutions, for their part, are skeptical of being exposed to the intellectual predilections and limitations of the single academic institution.

A variety of new approaches to university cooperation in Latin American development are being explored. The outright consortium, in which several universities are equal partners in an international program, tends to be viewed by the universities as administratively too complex.[3] A more acceptable variation places primary responsibility in a single institution with others participating as lesser partners. This is appealing to the university with the responsibility; it may be satisfactory if the roles of the other participants are limited and clearly specified. The Southwest Alliance for Growth, sponsored by the University of Oklahoma, in which nearly two dozen other institutions are participating, is illustrative of this type of consortium.

The agreement between the University of Chile and the University of California to cooperate in a variety of fields mobilizes the extensive resources of California's university system for international development work. It suggests a prototype for other state university systems. Another device, which has been used in Colombia, is the U.S. visiting committee, drawn from more than one university, which has responsibility for staffing a technical assistance, training and research program. The limitation in this arrangement is that it offers little opportunity to develop institutional capabilities in the United States since no single U.S. university has prime responsibility.

The Brookings Institution is perhaps the leading non-university research organization presently at work in Latin America. It is participating in political research in Colombia and also has assisted in public administration research and training programs in Venezuela. One of the advantages of the non-university research institute is its relative freedom to assemble a staff, for a particular

---

[3] A purely U.S. consortium devoted to research, initially supported by the Ford Foundation, is the Inter-University Research Program in Institution Building. In spite of the flexibility of the supporting foundation, this has been a complicated program to administer.

program, without being bound by restrictions of the kind which are essential to universities.

For certain technical aspects of public administration assistance (budgetary procedures; general organizational work; personnel administration; and tax, accounting, and customs work) AID uses its own personnel, contracts with other federal agencies for expert services, or employs specialists for limited periods. For such work the United States possesses a large pool of potentially available technicians not only in the federal government but in the states and cities as well. However, for the most part these technicians have not worked abroad and are inexperienced in adapting their skills to the foreign setting. They are, of course, largely unprepared for work in Latin America in terms of language and country orientation. The long-term solution to these limitations is to build into the preparation of persons going into public administration at least some of the orientation needed for work abroad. In the short run both AID and the universities will need to draw on the skills of this substantial body of technicians as has been done in the case of a training program operating between the Budget Office of New York State and the Ministry of Finance of Venezuela. A similar use of state officials is being achieved through a contract between the government of Chile and the government of the state of California for work in natural resource development.

As American universities develop regional or country expertise they should increasingly be prepared to offer orientation programs to government officials about to undertake foreign training and technical assistance assignments. Such orientation, accompanied by language training, will be most effective if offered in depth; the one- or two-week "briefing" is unlikely to be adequate.

In concluding this discussion of operational considerations, we may suggest that their effect is being felt in virtually all of the public administration development efforts under way in Latin America, but obviously in considerably differing degree and manner from country to country. The pressures for rapid development, the strength or weakness of political support accorded public administration development; the "style" of the individual country both inherently and in its relationships with the United States; the "style" of external assisting agencies (which may in fact vary little from country to country); the problems of communication and coordination; and the competence of indigenous as well as external institutions for development work—all contribute to national mosaics which make modernization in each country an essentially unique affair. It will be useful to keep this in mind as we turn attention to suggested action measures for public administration development.

V

The Elements of Action

Because of the wide range of social and economic problems which find their prime source of relief only through effective government action, we go beyond discussing basic and operational influences to proposals for an action program. This is risky, since prescriptions, in general, will have aspects of irrelevance for the particular situation; it might be considerably more so without the benefit of the succeeding commentaries which relate our proposals to Brazil, Chile, Peru, and Venezuela. Further, prescriptions by North Americans are unavoidably tinged with the influence of their experience, irrespective of how keen the desire to work from Latin American perspectives. On this latter score it can only be said that North American experience is not necessarily entirely irrelevant to Latin America. The reader must use his own good judgment in deciding what may be in point and what not.

Our action proposals suggest ways of addressing the fundamentals taken up in Chapter III: the processes of political socialization; the nature of the civic culture; the structure of government and some of its more important operations; and empirical studies as background to training as well as improvement in government practice. The proposals also speak, at least indirectly, to some of the operational influences discussed in Chapter IV—the need to keep perspective on the time-consuming nature of development; the essentiality of strong political support for public administration development; the communications and coordination problem; the necessity to build institutional strength in several directions.

In constructing our proposals for country public administration development we have followed the logic which would appear to govern creating an "ideal" program—first things first, such as top-level political support; and the orderly accumulation of facts and evidence. This is a logic of exposition and rationality rather than of reality.

Two regional proposals are offered to establish a Latin American clearing house on public administration programs and activities and a Latin American social science research council to encourage the growth of the social sciences.

We conclude with a brief review of the implications, as we see them, of this analysis for the programs of several organizations which are assisting in Latin American public administration development.

PROPOSED MEASURES TO BE TAKEN BY INDIVIDUAL COUNTRIES

Establishment of a National Council on the Public Service

The development of any country's public administration is of such importance to the processes of modernization, calls for so many immediate as well as long-range actions, and involves so many governmental, political, educational, civic, and private institutions that it requires the guidance of a superior leadership group. It is proposed, therefore that a national council on the public service or some comparable leadership body be established in each country.[1] Membership in the council might include leaders of the congress and other political leaders, the rectors of major universities, directors of institutes engaged in public service training and research, and labor and business spokesmen.

The council, or its equivalent, should preferably be inaugurated by the President under circumstances offering the widest possible publicity to the functions it will perform. These functions might include: taking a public position with respect to the importance of developing the national public administration as rapidly as pos-

---

[1] Such bodies are periodically used in the United States to provide guidance and broad leadership on issues of national importance. But they are not a purely North American device for mobilizing national sentiment. For example, in 1960, President Alberto Lleras created a National Agrarian Committee to formulate proposals for an agrarian reform law. The committee included representatives of the Roman Catholic church, the army, congress, the universities, and various other interest groups. Working under the leadership of Vice President Chaves Lleras, it proposed a draft law which was referred to the Cabinet and thence to the Congress. In a little more than a year's time the bill became law.

sible; developing current and long-term plans for strengthening the public administration; receiving periodic reports on the state of the public service and informing the public of progress and problems; and generally serving as the national voice for a vigorous, modernizing public administration. In addition to these activities the council might enchance the public service by giving, annually, a limited number of distinguished service awards to persons who have made outstanding contributions to the development of the nation's public administration and awarding public service fellowships to exceptionally competent young men and women for study antecedent to taking up careers in the public service.

Collection of Data and Fundamental Studies

Steps should be taken to make more readily available the data necessary for successful operation of public administration programs. In a good many countries public administration projects and programs are undertaken without an adequate assessment of existing experience and information. It may be relatively simple in some instances to review and assemble the significant available materials. But for the most part the effort will be time consuming and costly because of limited bibliographic resources and poor government documentation. For a single institution such as a university or research institute to take on the task of becoming an information center on public administration may be unduly burdensome without special funds, staff, and professional guidance. However, in a few countries there are already the beginnings of such centers, the Vargas Foundation in Brazil and CENDES in Venezuela, for example.

Considerable data needed for immediate operating purposes are collected for day-to-day operations by governments and their foreign consultants and advisers. However, much of this effort is ad hoc; it does not contribute to accumulating well-ordered, priority-related information. A principal source of guidance with respect to information which will be of most immediate as well as continuing significance may be the national development plan. In some instances, as for example with Peru and Guatemala, the national development plans contain diagnoses of major public administration problems which are deterrents to plan implementation. These suggest priorities for analysis and action.

Data and investigations which may be needed for operating purposes can include analyses of: manpower requirements for the public service and of the output of supply sources such as universities, foreign study programs, etc.; organization of the executive branch of the government including the Office of the Presidency; organization of functional activities such as agriculture, housing, education, transportation, etc.; budgetary processes including operating and capital budgets, relationship of budgets to planning system, methods of control, accounting and auditing procedures; public corporations including policy and administrative control, internal methods of operation, economic significance; local governments in terms of forms, authority, functions, financial relationships to higher governmental authorities; role of political parties; state, departmental, and regional governments including authority, functions, fiscal situation, political processes; the functioning of the bureaucracy, in particular civil service laws, procedures, pay schedules, and the status of public employment; governmental programs related to private sector development including licensing and import procedures, administration of tax benefits, and other inducements to investment.

Out of such an array of possible areas for data gathering and investigations, it is necessary to identify priority interests. Only in this way can the effort be kept relevant and within manageable bounds. Criteria for determining priorities may be found in the following situations: projects are under way, and additional data gathering and investigations are required to bring them to completion; projects identified in the development plan as having priority status require data gathering or operational research; projects needing prior operational research or data gathering are located in institutional settings having traditions, interests, and prior experience which suggest that progress can be made.

The assignment of responsibility and funds for the conduct of inquiries needed for operating purposes also calls for (1) identifying the institutions to be used, (2) fixing responsibility, and (3) determining the financial resources to be called upon.

Those investigations which are government-wide in scope or implication, e.g., manpower assessments, can usually be conducted most appropriately by an entity such as CENDES in Venezuela, which has general research responsibilities, by the Di Tella Institute, or by the Vargas Foundation. Specific administrative studies, which are still broad in scope, such as government-wide organizational appraisals of public corporations, of local governments, or of functional areas involving several agencies, may be conducted by a government institute such as ONRAP in Peru; under contract arrangement with an external organization such as the Public Administration Service of Chicago; or by a commercial management firm, in association with the national planning agency or an ONRAP-type institute. The government's own central statistical agency may be an important source of data as may be individual ministries and agencies.

The role of local universities will be modest with respect to operationally oriented investigations. However, as far as cooperative arrangements between government agencies and the universities permit, universities' involvement in data gathering can be significant to both scholars and practitioners in demonstrating the methods of empirical work.

Fundamental studies of government and the citizen are needed for long-term action and education programs. Little research of this type is presently under way in Latin America. The reasons are fairly apparent: the lack of social science tradition in the universities; the newness of the sociological concepts; the interests of scholars (primarily U.S.) in explorations in Asia, the Middle East, and Africa rather than Latin America; the limited number of present arrangements to permit sustained, cooperative research between U.S. and Latin American social scientists; and the paucity of funds to support such research.

Some of the types of fundamental inquiries that are needed are: (1) Studies of the ways in which citizens, in particular such strategic groups as political leaders, labor leaders, the "elite" bureaucracy, and youth leaders, have acquired their political values, ideas, and attitudes. (2) Studies of voting behavior and civic participation. (3) Studies of the political parties: their histories, organization, self-image, and modes of operation in the day-to-day governmental arenas. (4) Legal studies including the history of constitutional development, the character of legal education, the political role of the legally educated, the functioning of the law-enforcement system, and the organization and functions of courts. (5) Studies of legislative processes at all levels of government including organization and staffing of congress, composition of membership, party and interest group functions, relationships to executive and bureaucracy, to judiciary, and to military. (6) Studies of the Presidency including backgrounds of incumbents, role in political leadership, role in bureaucratic leadership, relationships to congress, courts, and military, relationships to other interest groups, external relationships with other Latin countries and the U.S., and roles in international agency activities.

With the exception of the purely historical investigations, most of the suggested studies are of a highly political character. They can be undertaken only if their importance is recognized and supported at appropriate leadership levels in the country. While competence to undertake historical research is fairly readily available, the other social science skills required frequently are not. Nor are many scholars available with experience in organizing and directing complex political or sociological investigations. Both Latin American and U.S. scholars and politicians are aware, from unhappy recent experience, of the hazards of conducting such fundamental research without full knowledge and support of the domestic political leadership. Yet the ability to do such work is to be found principally in U.S. universities and government research institutions. Latin American scholars must be trained for the task.

It is necessary, then, to conduct such research under well-specified conditions. There must be agreement at the highest levels of government that investigations of the kind suggested should be undertaken. Assuming such agreement, the arrangements for the conduct and support of such research should be spelled out quite fully. Since U.S. university personnel might well be involved, they should be given thorough preparation concerning the environment in which they will be working. Indeed, one objective of such research should be to build greater competence among U.S. scholars in Latin American affairs. Sponsorship of the project should be by a local institution such as the National Planning Agency. If foreign financial support is involved, the conditions should be fully understood. Field investigations would preferably be conducted by local scholars or students. Reports and publications derived from such studies should be disseminated locally.

The exact methods of developing a fundamental research program of this type will vary. Initiative may come from a university or a research institute. It may come from government quarters. Priorities must be set among research possibilities. The interest of government or university leaders in aspects of the civil culture, for example, would clearly offer a rationale for moving ahead in that area. Governmental concern with fundamental structural reforms might lead to a study of the presidency or the congress. A desire to strengthen political party operations, as expressed by several Latin American presidents in recent years, might be the decisive factor. Other influential considerations may be the research interests of local scholars, the research experience and interests of foreign scholars invited to participate, and the interests of funding organizations in the conduct of certain types of basic research.

Education and Training Activities

The support and development of institutions and programs which generate an understanding of public affairs and train for public service is clearly a central focus of attention. The scope ranges from civic education in the schools through university and postgraduate education to technical training for the practitioner. The development of political leadership, with its important educational aspects, is a special problem dealt with subsequently as a separate topic.

The interrelationships between programs of education and the problems discussed above hardly need elaboration. For educational and training purposes, background knowledge is invaluable both to identify educational needs and to supply the kind of factual information which permits meaningful instruction. Research, both operational and fundamental, goes hand in hand with education. The same personnel involved in research activities will nearly always also be engaged on the educational front. Institutions will usually be devoted both to research and education.

Three action steps are proposed: (a) appraisal of existing institutions and programs, (b) the further development of training programs with an immediate impact, and (c) the further development of educational programs with a long-term impact. Once again the intention is to indicate approaches and scope rather than precise patterns.

a.   The educational institutions, universities public and private, training institutes, schools of public administration, special programs carried on within research foundations, etc., are usually readily identifiable, at least in general terms. What is less familiar is the nature of courses and specialized curricula bearing on the public service offered by these institutions. Further, some types of courses and programs tend to be overlooked when the resources available for public service training and education are considered. Examples of these are found in military staff colleges, schools of business administration, faculties of medicine and law, schools of social work and nursing and other professional or vocational schools.

The task of listing and appraising the resources for education and training for public affairs is not overwhelming for most countries since so few exist. But for Brazil, with its large number of programs in public administration, its many universities and specialized institutes and programs, the effort is complex. In a subsequent section we suggest the establishment of a regional clearing house of information on public affairs. Given the uniqueness of Brazil, in size and language, it may be desirable that a Brazilian clearing house be created.

Another demanding task is to obtain sufficient information to judge whether specific programs are meeting the objectives for which they were created. A resource for doing this may be the external university or consortium. In relatively complex situations, another approach may be to obtain the services of a consultant or consulting firm. Since in several countries USAID has contracted with U.S. faculties, departments, or schools of education to study the Latin American educational system, such resources might be called upon.

If education and training programs for public affairs are to function and develop in a practicable manner, it is necessary to have some means of identifying deficiencies, setting priorities, and stimulating the growth of new or expanded activities.

b.   Programs of training of more or less immediate benefit are being carried on in most countries. These tend to be courses in clerical and management skills such as record keeping, office management, budgeting, organization and methods, accounting, and personnel administration. Sometimes such courses are offered as part of a series leading to a certificate; frequently they may be taken on an ad hoc basis. For the most part they reach lower and middle level personnel in the public service. Some of the types of training which are not widely offered and which hold promise of having an immediate impact are suggested here as likely new developments for country training programs.

Executive Conference Programs. Senior government officials in most of the countries under study are so pressed by the demands of their work that they seldom have an opportunity to reflect on either broad policy issues or major organizational arrangements. Executive conference programs, especially designed to accommodate these officials and to challenge their interests, can be important both in improving management practices and in enlarging policy contributions to government.

Such programs may be offered either through evening meetings or in weekend or five- to seven-day "residential" settings, preferably away from the seat of work. The conference subject matter can deal with broad problems of administration such as the relationships between the political processes and administration; between planning in ministries and central planning; the budget-planning nexus; organization of the presidency; and issues of the civil service such as uniform pay scales. The subject matter can also turn to questions of national policy: agricultural reform; population control; alternative strategies in educational policy; industrial development policy; and issues of national fiscal policy such as inflation, balance of payments, etc. Participants may be selected on the basis of position, e.g., permanent secretaries; or on the basis of common administrative or functional specialities, e.g., planning officials, economists, administrators of agricultural programs, of housing programs, etc. The executive conference approach may extend to audiences of legislators, jurists, governors, mayors, and other governmental leader groups after it is tried with senior officials of the executive branch.

Conferences for such senior officials require careful planning and the services of outstanding experts since they must be conducted with mature, sophisticated leadership. To assure success requires fixing responsibility for organizing and conducting the programs in the hands of highly competent individuals, a well-established institutional base (such as a university, institute, or research foundation), and sufficient financial resources to provide the proper expert assistance as well as an appropriate setting.[2]

Program to Attract Able University Students into the Public Service. One of the gravest problems is the low status connected with public employment everywhere in Latin America. Young people must be attracted to careers in the public service. The demands for trained personnel are great in all sectors, private as well as public, and governments do not offer competitive salaries. Further, the concept of public service is not well developed; there is little prestige or honor associated with public employment below the political level. Indeed the reverse tends to be true.

A program is suggested which would bring a small number of outstanding university students into public service on a study-internship basis during their last university year.[3] The student would be given a stipend or fellowship which would obligate him to take one or two courses related to the public service in one of the organizations training in public affairs. This could be done during the academic year; the stipend would permit freedom from outside employment and consequently time for the increased academic workload. Upon successful completion of the academic year the student would be given an internship of nine to twelve months, with a stipend for living expenses. If the assignment is carefully selected, for example if the intern works as a personal assistant to a minister, deputy minister, permanent secretary, or legislative leader, he will be exposed to the wide range of demanding and stimulating responsibilities which characterize high level positions in the public service. His permanent assignment, following completion of the internship, should be carefully selected to provide continual challenge. The student should also be promised the opportunity, if he is successful, to undertake a program of graduate study after approximately three years of service in the government. The graduate program would in most instances be

---

[2] The outstanding prototype is the well-known Executive Conference Programs offered by the Brookings Institution to U.S. public and business executives.

[3] An effort somewhat in this vein is being tried at INAD in Guatemala.

pursued in the United States or western Europe. Since it would be financed with public funds, it should carry a commitment to return to the public service or to a university, institute, or other organization with broad responsibilities for research and training in public affairs.

The planning and administration of a program of this type needs the cooperation of universities, public administration training organizations, and senior government officials. It may work most effectively if it is inaugurated by a national body such as the proposed national council on the public service.

In-Service Training Programs in Government Agencies. If such training is concentrated in organizations which are central to the country's socio-economic development program, the results may be particularly useful. The types of courses which can be offered under such circumstances tend to be limited to ones where teaching materials can be readily prepared in quantity and where the demands for preparation on the part of either instructors or students are not heavy. Illustrative are courses in accounting, introductory statistics, records management, typing, stenographic, and office management skills. To achieve the most immediate impact in terms of improving performance in clerical and management skills, training should be given in ministries and agencies during or immediately after working hours.

While at present relatively little training is conducted within ministries and agencies, the number of persons who might be reached could be greatly expanded if such training were offered. The central training institute, e.g., ONRAP, which gives such programs in its own offices, should perhaps modify its approach to concentrate on (a) the production of teaching materials for such courses and (b) the training of instructors who can conduct classes in the agencies. In some agencies where large numbers of persons need training in specific subjects, the instructor offering the first course can perhaps identify capable students who can take over the course for subsequent groups, under general supervision. In this manner there could be fairly rapid proliferation of government training.

Agencies are usually willing to pay for such training for their employees. While in some situations (Guatemala, for example) volunteer instructors have been used with some success by a central training institute, salaried teachers encourage more competent instruction, better morale, and tighter control by the responsible training organization.

Training of Local Government Personnel. Highly centralized government is characteristic of Latin America. While for purposes of socio-economic development there are marked advantages in having extensive powers at the center, with the growth of urbanism (Latin America is urbanizing faster than any other region of the world; about half its present population lives in urban centers) it becomes imperative that government programs be extended to the villages, towns, and cities and that able local officials be in charge. Problems of urban government, of course, go far beyond the competence of officials. Constitutional and legal questions, tax and fiscal policies, the distribution of services, and the operation of political parties are also involved.

As with in-service training for lower level administrative personnel in ministries and agencies, there is an opportunity to engage in extensive training of local officials on a decentralized basis. Present practice is either to train in a central institute or to offer courses at regional institutions or through ad hoc regional conferences and meetings. Conferences, especially, can be used to offer training to mayors, prefects, and other senior local or regional officials.

But for the large numbers of lower level administrators in local government offices, little is now offered. Since the functions of lower level administrators tend to be standardized and routine, it is possible to describe their work rather completely. This has seldom been done, but would not be a demanding task and would permit the preparation of self-instructional materials, carefully developed so that the trainee is led, step by step, through a course of instruction. Such materials can be printed in inexpensive booklets. The initial cost for the services of the data gatherers and programmers should be far less than the cost of traveling instructional teams.

While self-instruction has not been attempted in public administration in Latin America, the needs for training at the local government level appear to offer an ideal opportunity. Inauguration of such a program calls for a determination that this approach will be tried, and the allocation of responsibility and resources to conduct experimental work. The innovative nature of such a training scheme would perhaps lead to external support for the development of a trial program.

c. The expansion of education and training programs which will have a long-term influence is fundamental to the development of the public administration in each country. Some of the characteristics of current education with implications for public affairs have been suggested at various points in the preceding pages. In summary it can be said that there is virtually no evidence of efforts to develop an understanding of government and public affairs in the educational process beneath the university level.

While education is professionally oriented from the first or second year on, the public service as such is not identified as a career goal in the universities. Young people with political ambitions usually study in faculties of law. The rare individual who consciously aims for government service as a professional career will elect a faculty of law. Indeed, law is looked upon as the route into many respectable occupations which do not require other well-defined professional or advanced training.

The law faculties have shown few signs of developing courses which will prepare for public service. Constitutional and administrative law, the legal bases of such major elements of modernization as agricultural reform, urban development, the encouragement of foreign and domestic industrial development, and the newly emerging Common Market concern them very little. The impact of the law and law-enforcement administration on the citizen, and hence on his attitudes toward government and its agencies, is remote from legal education. There are limited signs of change but in only a few law faculties.

Earlier discussion of the state of the social sciences in Latin American universities indicated that with the exception of some faculties of economics, a few departments of sociology, and awakening departments of political science, there is little to prepare or inspire the student to consider a public service career. There are, however, modest opportunities for preparation for public service in the form of scholarships and fellowships to study abroad and in a very few instances to take postgraduate studies directed to public administration within Latin America. Foreign study awards are provided in a limited number of cases by individual governments, more often by USAID, the private foundations, and other governments, e.g., France. Training opportunities offered by the international agencies are primarily in the nature of specialized courses available to persons already in the public service.

In the following paragraphs we suggest a few of the directions in which countries may move for the long-term development of their educational resources to generate understanding, competence, and interest in public affairs.

Beyond pursuing some of the fundamental studies which have been discussed earlier, it would appear wise to appraise the present condition of civic education in the schools. Civic education of a developmental character in the primary and secondary schools receives little if any attention. It is probable that information about government and its role in society is presented largely in historical terms. Thus the oppressive and conflict-ridden aspects of government dominate. It may be assumed, also, that other governments are studied largely in terms of their relationship to Latin America with emphasis on themes of conflict and domination. The problem of introducing new elements into civic education in the schools is formidable. The societies of most countries are stratified, a condition which results in little traffic between classes. Students cannot learn from firsthand observation about how to participate in public affairs as in England and the United States.

An interesting experience would be to select a few schools and introduce new materials on the citizen's responsibilities in a democratic society, voting and political parties, civic behaviors in other countries, e.g., U.S., England, or U.S.S.R., on the socio-economic activities of the home government, the UN, the OAS, and the Alliance for Progress. In the upper levels of secondary schools it would be a salient experiment to introduce information about the career opportunities in public and private organizations involved in development efforts and the educational background needed for such careers.

Development of the social sciences in the universities has been identified as one of the very great needs in the long-term growth of competent personnel for the public service. Without further elaboration of this need, a few suggestions are offered which can lead to action. First, the impetus for the introduction of social science curricula must come from leadership within individual universities. The availability of foreign assistance or training opportunities for individuals interested in the social sciences will be wasted if there is not basic determination to improve and develop the field. Unless a rector or a dean of economics or law is eager to encourage the effort, the possibilities would not be promising. Second, one of the routes to demonstrating the relationships between social science education and public service training may be the formulation of some joint courses between institutes training for the public service and university faculties teaching sociology, economics, and political science. Third, the involvement of university faculty in the data gathering and functional research previously discussed may illuminate the utility of objective research, at least as it relates to public affairs.[4]

Given the central role of law faculties, attention should be directed to modernizing curricula and to expanding the experience, especially with the legal problems of modernization, of law faculty members. The same caveat applies, however: unless indigenous leadership is interested and takes initiative, little can be accomplished. Even with leadership, limited opportunities for study and observation of law, taught from the perspective of the sociology of modernization, pose difficulties in establishing programs of action.[5]

One of the important influences encouraging a consideration of the role of law in a changing economic environment comes from the Common Market in Central America. A few Latin American lawyers are considering the legal aspects of this new economic association, and we may assume that when the Common Market of South America begins to function, even more pressure will be felt. These situations may be examined through government programs of travel and observation for law faculty members. Governments may also find it desirable to involve law faculty members as consultants in important modernization programs to expose them to the legal issues involved as well as to have the benefit of their

[4] In this discussion and in succeeding paragraphs no mention is made of two widely known needs in Latin American higher education, (a) development of a core curriculum to provide at least a modicum of basic liberal arts training to each student and (b) a substantial increase in full-time faculty. These problems are important to education for public service.

[5] The program of the Inter-American Law Institute of New York University is designed to give young Latin American jurists a working knowledge of the American system of law—public, civic, and commercial. It also provides opportunities for observation of American legal systems in operation. The program is unique in the United States.

counsel. In at least a few instances, joint course development between institutes of business and public administration and faculties of law may have mutually beneficial results. Administrators need to become acquainted with the nature of legal thinking. The closeness of such institutes to the practical world of business and government would have useful repercussions in law faculties. Finally, the engagement of law faculty members in some of the data gathering and functional research which has been discussed above may encourage empirical approaches to the study of law.

University study abroad, despite problems of language, previous education, and general adjustment, remains one of the important means of educating the future scholar or practitioner of public affairs. While some countries have reasonably extensive information on the scholarships and fellowships available from public and private sources, this is not typically the case. Gathering such information is the essential first step to determining whether the government will further invest in foreign study opportunities. USAID, foundations, and the international agencies also need scholarship and fellowship information for their programs of support for study abroad.

The Extension of Technical Advisory Services

Technical advice about public administration to governments in Latin America comes from several sources and takes a variety of forms. Some governments have their own management advisory staffs in ministries of finance, budget offices, and planning agencies. Management advice may also be rendered by an institute or school of public administration. The number of experienced personnel in these management advisory units is very limited. The typical assistance given is on organizational problems within ministries and agencies.

The major source of technical advice on public administration is USAID. Working through contracts with U.S. management firms, nonprofit institutes, and universities; through direct employment of technicians; and through contracts with specialized agencies of the U.S. government (Internal Revenue Service, Customs Service, etc.), it provides a great variety of assistance. In recent years USAID has tended to concentrate a good deal of attention on tax and customs administration, but also has helped to organize planning offices and civil service administrations and to conduct overall government organization studies. It gives considerable support to agriculture, education, transportation, and housing; in the course of much of this work administrative problems are dealt with.

The United Nations supplies technicians in public administration, usually on an individual project basis as part of its larger public administration program. The BID and the World Bank, in approving loans for development projects, occasionally will specify that certain management problems be met. Thus limited portions of loan funds become available for technical advice on management issues.

While it is widely agreed that education and training are the fundamental keys to an improved public administration, many factors lead to emphasis on technical assistance. The ten-year goal of the Alliance for Progress, and the establishment of targets of development within that framework, is the most insistent reason for emphasizing projects for immediate administrative reform rather than long-term educational approaches. Yet there is evidence that such reform is frequently ineffective. In consequence, USAID is becoming interested in long-term arrangements with U.S. educational institutions for assistance in building the human resources needed for development. This approach, however, has not yet influenced some of AID's Latin American missions which continue almost exclusively to stress technical assistance.

It is obvious, of course, that technical advice is urgently needed for many purposes and that the countries cannot wait until more favorable circumstances are developed through educational processes. A few guidelines may be suggested to effect greater success in projects and programs of administrative reform.

First, sweeping endeavors which run counter to deeply entrenched social and economic conditions should be avoided. For example, efforts to introduce major civil service reform are likely to lead to frustration in situations where unemployment is high, patronage is essential to the maintenance of the governing party, a great paucity of skills characterizes the labor market, and no particular ethic exists about the public service or work in general. A much more modest effort to set standards of pay and basic qualifications for a limited number of strategic positions in the executive office of the president, the national planning agency, or some key development ministries may have a useful consequence.

Second, the appointment of an individual technician to work on complex problems, in an organization which is basically not committed to modernization, should not be encouraged. It is almost certain that the technician will feel frustrated and accomplish little.

Third, the technical assistance team with "formula solutions" that have succeeded in other countries should be viewed with skepticism. Similarly, technical assistance teams drawn from a single foreign institution which has a "doctrine" should preferably be augmented by technicians with other conceptual viewpoints.

Fourth, after agreeing to proposals for technical aid, the inclusion of training activities associated with that aid will produce more lasting results. Finally, while negotiating loans for development projects, the simultaneous request for resources in the form of administrative advice may assure greater effectiveness.

The typical pattern is to have responsibility for foreign aid fixed in the national planning agency. Thus the guidelines suggested above would, in most instances, be articulated through that organization. This suggests close collaboration between the governmental unit concerned with administrative management and the national planning agency. Another reason for such collaboration is that the management arm of the government needs advice on priorities, and this can best come from the planning agency. In all cases the requirements for management assistance outstrip the facilities available to provide help; obviously such help as is available ought to be directed to the most crucial points in the government, e.g., the executive office of the president, the planning agency itself, the budget office, congressional services, and agencies charged with priority responsibilities under the development plan.

Building a strong administrative management unit which can send technical assistance teams to work at these crucial points is likely to result in more administrative progress than is scattering management analysts in staff positions throughout ministries and agencies. A prime target of external technical assistance should thus be the central management unit. After this has been properly staffed and has acquired solid experience (often through participating in projects with management specialists from abroad) it may be possible to set up small liaision management staffs in key ministries and agencies. But such proliferation should be handled cautiously. Under optimum conditions, where decentralization of government services and development programs is becoming a reality, it would be desirable to establish management assistance units on a regional basis. This could be accomplished through branch offices of the central unit or through regional institutes of administration with both training and technical assistance responsibilities. But for most countries such schemes are well in the future.

The Development of Political Leadership

The improvement of a nation's public administration, as we noted earlier, is highly dependent on support from political leadership. Administrative change inevitably involves challenge to accepted modes of action and to traditional values and prerogatives. Projects for administrative reform, if they are other than routine and minor, must be backed by the president and his principal associates; preferably they will be supported by the congressional leadership as well.

But this is only part of the need in a program of action that is concerned with all governmental processes and which recognizes the very long-term nature of modernization. It is possible to suggest some of the steps that can be taken to aid the development of a better understanding of competent administrative performance on the part of a variety of contemporary political leaders. It is also necessary to think about future political leadership and the ways in which it can be prepared to assume responsibility. More than any other, political functions are of prime importance in modernizing societies. Even a superficial glance at the countries of Latin America will reveal that as the political leadership goes, so goes the entire development effort.

This profound yet obvious condition is one that tends to be confronted by most of the participants in Latin American development in a most oblique manner, and for good reasons. While various kinds of activities which bear on political development and leadership are suggested by USAID, foundations, and other external organizations, some of which are mentioned below, there is seldom if ever frank mutual exploration among the parties to Latin American development regarding the generation of new political leadership. The fact that some externally supported activity goes on, and that this subject is close to the source of success or failure for the Alliance for Progress would seem to warrant its receiving more open treatment.

Tradition in most countries suggests that political leadership is not something which is "trained for." It happens. And the process of its happening is viewed as the private affair of each nation, not to be meddled in by others. Our action proposals in this area are suggestions as to how political education may begin to receive consideration in appropriate quarters.

Political leadership emerges from a great many sources in Latin America: the political parties themselves; the military; the business community; groups which by virtue of family position, wealth, tradition, and education have played dominant roles in politics; youth and student organizations; the church; and labor and agrarian institutions. A good deal of USAID's concern with the development of political leadership has been to give to individuals drawn from such sources an opportunity for travel and observation, particularly in the United States. AID has also supplied foreign advisers, materials, and equipment to key groups which are presumed to be significant from the point of view of leadership. A great many other AID-supported activities have an indirect bearing on the development of political leadership: school and university development efforts; work with cooperatives and labor unions; community development projects; adult education; urban development; agricultural reform; and public administration education and training.

Loyola University, under contract with USAID, gives seminars to young leaders from Central America. The core program offers studies in the economics of development, social and psychological aspects of change, political problems of development, the role of political leadership, etc.

The American Institute of Free Labor Development, a U.S. nonprofit organization, conducts a variety of training programs for young labor leaders both in Washington, D.C., and in countries abroad. Its training emphasis is on the fundamentals of union leadership, organizing techniques, tactics for dealing with corruption and extremism, as well as on basic economics, labor-management relationships, etc. The Institute is under the policy guidance of a Board of Trustees made up of both North and Latin Americans, a majority of whom are trade union representatives. Others are public figures and progressive business executives. It is supported in part by USAID and in part by labor and other private sources.

The Institute of International Labor Research (IILR) has been trying for several years to identify, train, and organize leadership of the agrarian political sector in Latin America. Its first program in political education was in organizing the Institute of Political Education in San José, Costa Rica. It ran a number of courses between 1959 and 1962 for students recruited from liberal and progressive political parties throughout Latin America. The curriculum covered such fields as history, sociology, the ideology and organization of political parties, economic development, and international affairs. Among other interesting conclusions drawn from this experience were that the major vacuum in political leadership is at the second and third levels rather than at the top; that leadership should be determined by a process of natural selection rather than by appointment; that training programs must keep goals clearly in mind; and that country differences make the regional approach far less useful than programs designed for individual countries or sub-regions.

The IILR also ran an Inter-American Center for Political Training (CIDAP) in the Dominican Republic and, in 1962, organized a Center for Social Research and Documentation (CEDS) in Mexico.

Through its Foreign Policy Studies Division, the Brookings Institution is involved in a long-range research program on political development in modernizing countries, with special emphasis on Latin America. It has probably gathered more information on activities directed toward political development in Latin America than any other organization in the United States, and is thus an important factual resource.

In Colombia, in recent years the Ford Foundation and USAID personnel took part in a series of seminars which brought together young political leaders, scholars, and managers to consider national public policy issues. These so-called Public Affairs Seminars are a largely untried but relatively simple means of enlarging understanding on the part of young leaders and of bringing them into communication with one another.

The International Development Foundation, a private nonprofit organization with headquarters in New York, is concerned with the development of political leadership. One of its most successful programs is in Peru where about one thousand university students, after orientation in techniques of community development and in relevant background materials, are sent to work annually in the Indian villages of the Altaplana during their summer vacations. This indigenous Peruvian "peace corps" is exposing a substantial number of potential future leaders of the country to an area and population that have traditionally been ignored and neglected by the educated elite.

From the viewpoint of a strengthened and modernized public administration, the fundamental question of political leadership has two aspects. First is the matter of its development, its values and perspectives, and ultimately its goals and methods. These are questions geared to the future; the state of the public administration in twenty years will depend very much on what kind of political leadership is in the making today. Second is the more immediate question of how the current political leadership can learn about the importance of public administration to modernization. The action suggestions which follow deal with these matters in reverse order.

Preparations for immediate action might include some of the following:

a. Short seminars on the development of political leadership in the country, the significance of political support for the modernization of public administration, and the present programs of public administration development. The audiences for the seminars might be groups of (1) key legislators, (2) party leaders from the principal parties, (3) ministers or deputies, (4) business and industrial leaders, (5) labor leaders, (6) military leaders, (7) university faculty, especially from law schools, and (8) journalists. These seminars could be offered by a university, an institute of administration, or a specially organized conference on political development. Support for such an effort might be obtained from local or external foundations. The sources of financial support should be above suspicion of self-interest or bias. The planning and conduct of the seminars would necessitate a limited amount of background research and conceivably could be useful in stimulating research on political leadership.

b. In training programs in business and public administration, and in military staff college programs, where mid-career training is offered, encouragement to consider the relationships between political leadership and modernization, including public administration especially. The use of external consulting assistance may be particularly helpful in applying perspectives and experience from other countries, as well as the results of other research.

Measures which have as their goal the influencing of long-term development of political leadership might include some of the following types of efforts:

a. The development of a fellowship-internship program, probably in cooperation with a domestic and a U.S. university, for about half a dozen able university graduates to study for a Master's degree in a U.S. school of politics. This would be followed by an internship at home in the executive office of the president, a governor or mayor, or as an aide to the head of a major political party.

b. Encouragement of the introduction into the education and training programs of university faculties, schools, military institutes, etc., of course materials on political history, operation of the political parties, and relationships between politics and development, and the encouragement of complementary research programs.

c. Stimulation of the introduction into public and private secondary schools of elementary materials on politics, parties, and the relationships between socio-economic development and politics.

d. Encouragement of the introduction of objective information on political parties, the bureaucracy and its development, and the citizens' political responsibilities as a part of training which precedes civic action programs, where local troops are used for literacy training, health services, construction of schools, roads, etc.

e. Consideration of the establishment of a special School for Political Leadership which would bring together young people of already demonstrated leadership skills, from the universities, labor unions, agrarian reform, and other developmental government agencies, business communities, churches, etc., to study the government's development plans, economic policy in relationship to the plans, the administrative problems of development, the structure and functioning of the political parties, the congress, the executive, and the roles of personal and institutional leadership in national development.[6]

f. Encouragement of a domestic "peace corps" program with the goal of showing to educated young people problems and areas of their country which they otherwise might never know intimately. Candidates should be drawn from potential leadership sources, as is now being done in Peru.

g. Consultation with external supporting agencies interested in political development about the ways in which their various programs, such as study and travel awards for political leaders and work with labor and youth groups, may be related to domestic needs and current activities.

PROPOSED MEASURES OF A REGIONAL NATURE

Establishment of a Latin American Center of Public Affairs

We have earlier noted the inadequacy of communications and coordination with respect to public administration research, training, and practice. The evidence suggests that the creation of an information center which in time can take on other functions of a regional character, will be a useful investment.[7]

Several organizations theoretically might assume the clearing house function. For example, the International Institute of Administrative Sciences (IIAS) with headquarters in Brussels, Belgium, has as its objectives, ". . . formulating and disseminating the general principles of public administration, comparing the experience of different countries in this field, preparing adequate methods and, in general, surveys, studies, projects and agreements for the im-

---

[6] The experience of the former Institute of Political Education in San José, Costa Rica, should be examined in this connection.

[7] An examination of the experience of the Public Administration Clearing House of Chicago, 1930–56, is instructive with respect to the functions of the proposed center. Of relevance also is the Eastern Regional Organization for Public Administration (EROPA), with headquarters in Manila. EROPA has state, institutional, and individual memberships, runs conferences and seminars, has an information and research center, and operates a training center.

provement of administrative science and practice; (and serving as) an important center for international documentation on administrative matters. . . ." The fact that IIAS is based in Europe, that it has a world-wide membership, and that it is committed to concepts of administration as science suggests that it cannot provide the openness of approach and intensive focus on Latin America which is needed at this time.

The Council on Higher Education in the American Republics (CHEAR) is designed to bring officials of North and Latin American universities together to consider common problems. Its purposes are indirectly related to those foreseen for the center for public affairs. But CHEAR's focus on universities rather than public affairs would seem to preclude it from serving as a clearing house. Education and World Affairs is considering establishing a clearing house of information relevant to U.S.-Latin American higher education; it has already done this for Mexico, but again the focus is different.

The Economic Commission for Latin America, as has been noted, is developing public administration activities at its Santiago headquarters. The BID-supported FLACSO in Santiago and the Inter-American School of Public Administration in Rio de Janeiro are the sites of graduate programs in public administration. Any of these could presumably take on the clearing house task. So, too, could the Organization of American States. Whatever the sources of support, international agencies, private foundation funds, US-AID, or other, we believe the center for public affairs will need to have considerable flexibility with its funds in the early stages of developing its program.

The organization and operational aspects of the center can be sketched here only in general terms. Perhaps, on the initiative of a small group of interested Latin Americans, an exploratory meeting could be held to consider the scope of activity of the proposed organization and the means to organize and finance it. There should probably be a self-perpetuating board of trustees composed of about a dozen distinguished public figures drawn from different countries of Latin America, but not serving as country representatives. Through rotation of trustee terms each country should be able, during a five-year period, to have at least one distinguished citizen serve on the board. The board should select an outstanding Latin American with a wide acquaintance in Latin American public administration institutions and among the leaders of public affairs to serve as executive director.

It is suggested that the headquarters be located in a strategic city in Spanish-speaking Latin America. The environment would be most favorable in a situation where indigenous public affairs activities are prospering and where there are relatively strong public administration institutions, e.g., Caracas, Lima, or Santiago. It may be useful initially to have the center housed, for administrative convenience, in an existing institution like CORDIPLAN, ONRAP, or INSORA. Considering the size of Brazil and its language difference, a Brazil center might be established in Rio de Janeiro or Brasília, with its own director. The Vargas Foundation offers a logical physical location for a Brazil center.

The functions of the center will evolve over time. Suggested below are a number of activities which might be expected to become aspects of its program.

a. Factual information is needed on educational and training programs in each country. The focus can be on courses, seminars, degree or certificate programs, in-service training, executive development, and other educational activities designed to prepare persons for public service or to strengthen the capacities of those in public service.

In addition to gathering factual information on course content, institutional arrangements, numbers and types of students, instructors, and special features of programs, e.g., internships or field observation, an objective evaluation needs to be made of how well training is serving purposes it was designed to meet.

b. A similar appraisal needs to be made of each of the regional training programs operating in the field of public administration in Latin America.

c. An assessment is needed of the public administration library resources available in each country, and in regional institutions. A librarian from a leading Latin American public administration program might be invited to undertake this task. Efforts should be made to identify unusual materials, important works available in Spanish and Portuguese, materials needing translation, etc. The immediate goal might be a report which indicates the character of each collection, the identification of special problems, needs and opportunities, and recommendations as to how to maintain continuous reporting of significant library developments. As a part of this effort a review of the Latin American journals of administration would be useful, with substantive and geographic area gaps identified.

d. A survey of research in progress related to public administration, broadly conceived, should be undertaken. The scope of research suggested in this essay may serve as a basis for planning the survey. Means should also be devised for the continuous reporting of research in progress, perhaps in cooperation with the journal, *The Latin American Research Review.*

e. Technical assistance and advice is being offered in nearly all countries under a variety of arrangements and by many institutions, domestic and external. Information needs to be kept current on technical assistance efforts of significance, including scope of projects, agencies rendering assistance, funding, etc.

f. A manpower roster should be developed which ultimately would provide catalogued information on manpower skills needed for the various public administration functions. A separate roster of U.S. personnel with linguistic skills and Latin American experience might be considered. Study should also be given to compensation problems involved in using personnel for teaching and technical assistance across national lines in Latin America. Is a regional equalization scheme called for? If so, how might it operate?

g. Special projects.

From time to time the center might be requested by an international body such as the OAS, BID, UN, a foundation or government, to undertake a special project. A few of these are suggested to illustrate the kinds of activities which might be feasible for this organization.

1) A program of seminars for Latin American journalists to inform them about problems and progress with respect to Latin American public administration and to put them in a position to write feature articles for their newspapers. Public administration and the needs of the public service receive little attention in the press. A well-planned program, with field trips to successful gov-

ernmental and educational developments, could do much to arouse journalistic interest. The radio and television media should also participate.

2) A conference to consider the subject of political leadership development. This, however, is a sufficiently delicate task so that it should be undertaken only with appropriate sponsorship and support.

3) The general supervision of a series of public administration cases to be developed for teaching purposes with the objective of obtaining cross-regional comparisons.

4) General supervision of experimental work in the application of new teaching techniques in public service training programs, where regional experimentation is desired.

5) Evaluation of curricula, on a regional basis, in public service and related fields such as law, public health, and social work.

6) Appraisal of the services available to legislatures and congresses, e.g., legislative research services, library facilities, staff assistants, etc., where a regional survey may provide data of value in inaugurating intra-country improvements.

7) Study of new developments in local government, with the objective of disseminating information on the more successful practices, e.g., the Venezuela Foundation for Community Development and Municipal Improvement.

8) A survey of available statistical resources on a national and regional basis, and survey of major statistical series which are regularly available.

h. Improved communications is at the heart of the proposed center's operation. The development of a variety of media, e.g., a monthly newsletter, special reports, monographs, etc., as well as a roster, institutional and individual, of persons to receive the publications, would appear to be of strategic importance.

In concluding these suggestions, it is not anticipated the Latin American center for public affairs would become either (a) a regional training center, (b) a regional research center, or (c) an action agency to provide technical assistance. We doubt the feasibility, except for decidedly special purposes of establishing more regional training or research programs. While the center might, in time, provide technical assistance services, the first efforts should be concentrated on meeting communications and coordination needs of public administration in Latin America.[8]

Establishment of a Latin American Social Science Research Council (SSRC)

The development of greater capability in Latin American universities and research institutes to conduct empirical research, as well as to train in the social sciences, is, as we have earlier indicated, fundamental to the long-run strengthening of public administration. A Latin American Social Science Research Council would serve much broader academic interests than those related to public administration. But in Latin America linkages are needed between the scholarly institutions and the practitioner-oriented public affairs world within and close to government. A Latin American SSRC, we believe, can provide indirect but significant aid in creating such connections.

To implement the proposals in this essay, U.S. universities should deepen their knowledge of Latin American affairs. Unique among universities throughout the world, they possess the fundamental grounding in the social sciences which Latin America so sorely needs. If collaborative efforts can at the same time strengthen knowledge of Latin America in U.S. institutions and can build social science capabilities in Latin America, the objectives sought here will be well served. Some of the proposals with respect to the SSRC indicate directions of such efforts.

In the subsequent discussion of public administration in Venezuela, George Sutija describes the progress made through late 1966 in establishing a Latin American Social Science Research Council. These developments offer promise of bringing such an organization into being in the near future. Our own observations lead us to sug-

---

[8] In November, 1967, a conference on the role of universities in education for public administration was held in Rio de Janeiro under the joint auspices of the Vargas Foundation and the Latin American Development Administration Committee of the American Society of Public Administration. A principal conclusion of the conference was that clearing-house arrangements are urgently needed to assure exchange of information about public administration and training.

gest that the program of this SSRC might include activities of the following types:

a. Provision for advanced training in selected disciplines for a limited number of young social scientists, particularly those in universities where interests exist in developing the applicant's discipline. The training will ordinarily, but not inevitably, be taken in the United States.

b. Establishment of a limited number of committees to assess promising research opportunities in selected fields. Committees may be particularly useful in areas where Latin American social science research needs and interests can be joined with U.S. interests. They may also be of particular significance if they give attention to issues like political socialization or law and modernization which are basic to development and have implications for all of the nations of Latin America.

c. Inauguration of a conference program tied to the work of the committees particularly to encourage exploration by U.S. and Latin American social scientists of mutual research problems and interests.

d. Provision of individual grants to experienced scholars particularly in those areas where committee work has revealed promising opportunities.

e. Publication of a quarterly newsletter or bulletin similar to the U.S. SSRC, *Items.*

f. Cooperation in and, if necessary, support of Spanish and Portuguese editions of the *Latin American Research Review,* perhaps with special sections added to these editions.

g. Development of plans for a roster, by disciplines, of social science manpower resources in Latin America. In this connection consultation with the United States National Science Foundation may be useful.

IMPLICATIONS OF THIS ESSAY FOR CERTAIN EXTERNAL ORGANIZATIONS

A reading of the foregoing suggests certain program developments and modifications which are briefly referred to.

United States universities will almost certainly respond to the opportunity to engage in long-term development of their capacities for training and research on Latin American affairs, and for joining in collaborative programs with institutions in Latin America, if the resources are made available. They have responded in other fields —African and Asian studies, and science and engineering, for example. But U.S. universities require resources for exploration of a potential field, area, or discipline, and then need both funds and a mandate from the organization (most frequently the U.S. government), restricted only by broad administrative guides and broad program objectives. Under such circumstances it may be expected that over the next decade at least fifteen to twenty U.S. universities could become strong centers of Latin American studies, each with a regional or country emphasis.

USAID's mode of operation regarding public administration development in Latin America might be substantially modified if proposals in this essay are pursued. At the heart of AID's working relationship with U.S. universities and other non-governmental institutions is an assumption that the Alliance for Progress, in terms of U.S. obligations, is basically a governmental responsibility. The recognition that this endeavor must involve the participation of many non-governmental bodies, not simply their purchased services, has yet to become a part of congressional and AID philosophy.

Certain modifications in AID operations which would be useful in furthering objectives discussed in this essay are:

a. A gradual shifting of emphasis from short-term U.S. university contracts with very specific requirements for training and technical assistance to long-term contracts of a "block-grant" type which are country- or region-directed and which provide adequate resources for field work to develop Latin American regional competence on the part of U.S. faculty and graduate students. Such contracts should encourage research related to fundamental needs for knowledge about Latin America. Contracts might in some instances employ consortia arrangements.

b. Less emphasis on technical assistance projects and more on support of programs to assist in the gradual establishment of competent, well-staffed, central administrative management units in each country.

c. The development of programs, in cooperation with U.S. universities, to provide language and country or regional orientation to federal, state, and local government technicians who can become a major resource for technical advice in Latin America. In association with this development there should be exploration of ways to facilitate the *continuing* use of AID or contractor personnel with substantial Latin American experience.

The foundations are generally operating in a manner consistent with the approaches suggested in this essay. There is some tendency, because of very limited resources in foundations for work in Latin America, to direct efforts to "strategic spot jobs," rather than to think through broad strategy and to work in cooperation with AID and other external institutions in the pursuit of the components of strategy. In aproaches involving such cooperation, the foundation contribution might be to support the innovative, the experimental, and the politically difficult but strategically significant elements in a program.

Those organizations with region-wide interests and responsibilities, notably the UN, the OAS, and the BID, may find it particularly effective to support three types of efforts, each of which will be strategic to long-term public administration development:

1) the proposed Latin American Center of Public Affairs,

2) the Latin American social science research council, and

3) an expanded program of scholarships and fellowships for study abroad, or in Latin American educational institutions, with special emphasis on the social sciences and on subjects of relevance directly to meeting public administration needs.

The World Bank in its country studies may, with great benefit, extend its practice of associating public administration experts with its investigative teams and of having administrative issues identified in its reports.

We turn now to analyses of public administration in Brazil, Chile, Peru, and Venezuela and a consideration of certain of the ideas in this essay as they apply to developments in those countries.

References

This set of references is divided into two sections. Section A makes no attempt to list comprehensively the increasingly heavy volume of literature related to development administration but instead includes those individual works most useful in the preparation of this essay. Compiled by use of the same criterion, Section B is a listing of bibliographies.

A. INDIVIDUAL WORKS

Almond, Gabriel A., and James S. Coleman (editors). *The Politics of the Developing Areas*. Princeton, N.J.: Princeton University Press, 1960.

Almond, Gabriel A., and Sidney Verba. *The Civic Culture*. Princeton, N.J.: Princeton University Press, 1963.

Apter, David E. *The Politics of Modernization*. Chicago: University of Chicago Press, 1965.

Asher, Robert E., *et al. Development of the Emerging Countries: An Agenda for Research*. Washington, D.C.: The Brookings Institution, 1962.

Banfield, Edward C. *The Moral Basis of a Backward Society*. Glencoe, Ill.: The Free Press, 1958.

The Brookings Institution. *Political Development*. Reprint No. 65. Washington, D.C.: The Brookings Institution, 1962.

————. *Prepared Papers for Symposium on Research Needs Regarding the Development of Administrative Capabilities in Emerging Countries*. Conducted for the Agency for International Development by the Advanced Study Program. Washington, D.C.: The Brookings Institution, 1965 (see especially papers by Joseph La Palombara and Milton Esman).

Easton, David. *A Framework for Political Analysis*. Englewood Cliffs, N.J.: Prentice-Hall, 1965.

Education and World Affairs. *The University Looks Abroad: Approaches to World Affairs at Six American Universities*. New York: Walker and Company, 1965.

Gardner, John W. *A.I.D. and the Universities*. Washington, D.C.: Agency for International Development, 1964.

Guthrie, George M., and Richard E. Spencer. *American Professions and*

Overseas Technical Assistance. University Park, Pa.: Pennsylvania State University, 1965.

Harbison, Frederick, and Charles A. Myers. *Education, Manpower and Economic Growth: Strategies of Human Resource Development.* New York: McGraw-Hill, 1964.

Harbison, Frederick, and Charles A. Myers (editors). *Manpower and Education: Country Studies in Economic Development.* New York: McGraw-Hill, 1965.

Heady, Ferrel, and Sybil L. Stokes (editors). *Papers in Comparative Public Administration.* Ann Arbor, Mich.: The University of Michigan, 1962.

Johnson, John J. *The Military and Society in Latin America.* Stanford, Calif.: Stanford University Press, 1964.

Katz, Saul M. "Guia para Modernizar la Administracion para el Desarrollo Nacional." Paper read before the Inter-American Conference on Development Administration, Buenos Aires, Argentina, December, 1965.

Kriesberg, Martin (editor). *Public Administration in Developing Countries.* Washington, D.C.: The Brookings Institution in cooperation with the Advanced School of Public Administration, Bogotá, 1965.

La Palombara, Joseph (editor). *Bureaucracy and Political Development.* Princeton, N.J.: Princeton University Press, 1963.

————. "Public Administration and Political Change: A Theoretical Overview" (unpublished paper).

Lieuwen, Edwin. *Arms and Politics in Latin America.* Rev. ed. New York: Council on Foreign Relations by Frederick A. Praeger, 1961.

————. *Generals vs. Presidents: Neomilitarism in Latin America.* New York: Frederick A. Praeger, 1964.

Martindale, Don (editor). *Functionalism in the Social Sciences: The Strength and Limits of Functionalism in Anthropology, Economics, Political Science, and Sociology.* Monograph No. 5. Philadelphia: The American Academy of Political and Social Science, February, 1965.

McClelland, David C. *The Achieving Society.* Princeton, N.J.: Van Nostrand, 1961.

"Political Socialization: Its Role in the Political Process," *The Annals,* Vol. 361. American Academy of Political and Social Science (September, 1965).

Pye, Lucian W. (editor). *Communications and Political Development.* Princeton, N.J.: Princeton University Press, 1963.

————. *Politics, Personality, and Nation Building: Burma's Search for Identity.* New Haven, Conn.: Yale University Press, 1962.

Riggs, Fred W. *Administration in Developing Countries: The Theory of Prismatic Society.* Boston: Houghton Mifflin Company, 1964.

————. *The Ecology of Public Administration.* Bombay: Asia Publishing House, 1961.

Robinson, Mary E. *Education for Social Change: Establishing Institutes of Public and Business Administration Abroad.* Washington, D.C.: The Brookings Institution, 1961.

REFERENCES   85

Swerdlow, Irving (editor). *Development Administration: Concepts and Problems.* Syracuse: Syracuse University Press, 1963.
Thurber, Clarence E. "Islands of Development." Paper read before the Latin American Development Administration Committee of the Comparative Administrative Group, American Society for Public Administration, Washington, D.C., 1965.
Wagley, Charles (editor). *Social Science Research on Latin America.* New York: Columbia University Press, 1964.
Ward, Robert E., *et al. Studying Politics Abroad: Field Research in the Developing Areas.* Boston: Little, Brown and Company, 1964.
Weidner, Edward W. *Technical Assistance in Public Administration Overseas: The Case for Development Administration.* Chicago: Public Administration Service, 1964.

B. BIBLIOGRAPHIES

Gittinger, J. Price, and August Schumacher. "Development Planning Bibliographies." Prepared at the request of the Committee on National Planning Research of the American Society for Public Administration (Comparative Administration Group [CAG]) (mimeographed).
Harvard Law School. *Bibliography on Taxation in Underdeveloped Countries.* Cambridge: The Law School of Harvard University, 1962.
Hazlewood, Arthur. *The Economics of "Under-Developed" Areas: An Annotated Reading List of Books, Articles, and Official Publications.* London: Oxford University Press, 1954.
Heady, Ferrel, and Sybil L. Stokes. *Comparative Public Administration: A Selective Annotated Bibliography.* 2nd ed. Ann Arbor: The University of Michigan, 1960.
Institute of Public Administration. *Selected References Pertaining to Public Administration.* New York: Institute of Public Administration, 1965.
Katz, Saul M., and Frank McGowan. *A Selected List of U.S. Readings on Development.* Prepared for the United Nations Conference on the Application of Science and Technology for the Benefit of the Less Developed Areas. Washington, D.C.: Agency for International Development, 1963 (annotated).
Mars, David, and H. George Frederickson. *Suggested Library in Public Administration: With 1964 Supplement.* Los Angeles: University of Southern California, 1964.
Ministry of Overseas Development. *Public Administration: A Select Bibliography.* 1st supplement. Ministry of Overseas Development (Great Britain), 1964.
Simpson, Keith, and Hazel C. Benjamin. *Manpower Problems in Economic Development: A Selected Bibliography.* Princeton, N.J.: Industrial Relations Section, Princeton University, 1958 (annotated).

Spitz, Allan A., and Edward W. Weidner. *Development Administration: An Annotated Bibliography.* Honolulu: East-West Center Press, 1963.

U.S. Department of State. *Development Administration and Assistance: An Annotated Bibliography.* Washington, D.C.: Agency for International Development, 1963.

Commentaries

Brazil

PETER D. BELL

INTRODUCTION

The Honey essay does not itself constitute an operational strategy for public administration development; it contains "suggestions to be explored rather than formulas to be applied." The objective of this commentary is to evaluate the observations and recommendations of the essay in terms of both needs and possible courses of action in Brazil. Examining the suggestions in the general context of the Brazilian experience will not result in an operational strategy; the presentation of such a strategy would require the specific identification of agents to put the ideas into practice and of financial sources to support the strategy. The intent is to clarify the Brazilian situation and elaborate upon Honey's suggestions, applying his ideas concerning administration in Latin America to Brazil.

THE ADMINISTRATIVE SITUATION

The Development Demands

In a developing country such as Brazil, in which some 60 per cent of new investments are being made by the government, expectations for economic development are inextricably linked to the effectiveness of the public administration. The Brazilian bureaucracy, founded to maintain law and order in an agrarian society, is now faced with the more difficult responsibilities of encouraging industrial development and providing economic protection.

The process of national industrialization and expansion of the Brazilian domestic market has imposed new demands on the government. In the 1930's, new Ministries of Labor, Industry and

Commerce, Education and Health, and Aeronautics were created, as well as a rash of state *autarquias* (independent regulatory agencies) and mixed enterprises. Since World War II, each succeeding administration has been compelled as a matter of political survival to support economic development, and a major concomitant of governmental support has been national planning.

A relatively large and decentralized administrative bureaucracy is being faced with increased responsibilities. Some 292,000 civil functionaries were employed in the "centralized administration"[1] in October, 1965, according to an estimate by the Department of the Public Service (DASP). The number of federal employees would probably approach one million with the inclusion of all the employees of the *autarquias* and mixed enterprises who make up the "decentralized administration." These estimates do not take into account the several regional, twenty-one state, and more than four thousand municipal administrations. Nearly 90 per cent of those presently engaged in public administration were admitted outside of the legally compulsory examination system and thereby continue to be suspect of nepotism, favoritism, and clientelism. This sprawling public administration is being asked to execute increasingly complex and technical functions, and the cost of mistakes rises constantly.

Administrative Problems

A recent study of the Venezuelan bureaucracy revealed the presence of a sizable number of "risk-taking, innovative, optimistic, politically efficacious" young university graduates.[2] Similar individuals may be found in the Brazilian bureaucracy. They are undoubtedly among the "work-horse" groups described by two visiting professors from the University of Southern California as the small clusters of public servants in the Brazilian ministries and agencies, who, regardless of statutory position or formal authority,

[1] This term is used to refer to the executive branch of the government. Most of these 292,000 functionaries are employed by the sixteen ministries.
[2] See José A. Silva Michelena, "The Venezuelan Bureaucrat," in Frank Bonilla and J. A. Silva Michelena (eds.), *Studying the Venezuelan Polity: Explorations in Analysis and Synthesis* (MIT-CENDES, May, 1966).

accept the responsibility for getting the work of government done.[3] These freewheeling individuals and work-horse groups operate despite the general conditions of the public administration. Low wage levels in the public sector create problems. According to a recent Vargas Foundation study, the real wages of government *técnicos* deteriorated by 34 per cent between 1945 and 1964, despite salary adjustments for inflation. Because of the low salary levels the more energetic individuals seek part-time jobs, thereby dividing their energy and obligations among various locales and activities and detracting from their effectiveness at their government posts. Only the less energetic or skilled are satisfied with full-time employment at a single government job; these employees are frequently the ones who consider their position a sinecure and feel that the government, or their friends and relatives who have power in the government, owe them a position.

Another problem is absenteeism. In Bahia, for example, the Institute of Public Service recently surveyed the state government and came up with the remarkable estimate that 30 per cent of the employees on the public payroll never appear at work.

The merit system, required by state laws and constitutions as well as federal, is generally shunned in practice. Article 186 of the Federal Constitution of 1946 requires that "initial entry to career positions be through public examinations as established by law." In fact, only about 10 per cent of such positions have been filled by examination. Although the practice is illegal, legislatures frequently blanket into career positions political nominees originally appointed to fill temporary posts. One such group of *interinos* in Bahia recently celebrated a mass for the entire membership of the State Legislative Assembly. The legislature had suspended the state constitution, cancelled entrance examinations, and changed the political appointments of the *interinos* into career positions.

Administrative procedures are slow. Although the Constitution of 1946 (Art. 36) guarantees "the rapid pace of procedures in

[3] See John Rood and Frank Sherwood, "The Workhorse Group in Brazilian Administration," in *Perspectives of Brazilian Public Administration* (Los Angeles: The School of Public Administration, University of Southern California, June, 1963).

the public agencies and offices" and "expedition in the steps required for defense of the law," Brazilian administrative practice has been less than expeditious. For example, in 1966 the Supreme Court heard a case which had originally been referred to it in 1888, and cases commonly remain undecided by the Court for ten years or more. A professor from Minas Gerais related his experience in waiting a decade for a tax refund procedure to run its course. When the money was finally returned, the professor made the grand gesture of donating the sum to the state. The functionary making the refund, however, pleaded with him to keep his money, which had been reduced by inflation to a mere pittance, in order to spare the state another lengthy procedure. Examples of such delays in government proceedings could be multiplied.

The Reform Efforts

Brazilian governments since the 1930's have made attempts to remedy the ineffectiveness of the public administration. Getúlio Vargas emphasized the need for efficiency in government. Jânio Quadros, too, emphasized efficiency and honesty in government, riding to presidential power on a broomstick, the campaign symbol that he used to signify his intent to sweep corruption out of Brazil. Castello Branco showed an almost puritanical concern for the moral and economic aspects of the public administration. On several occasions in recent decades, this attention has resulted in legislation and decrees of major reforms, but these reforms have not been vigorously implemented.

A professor in the Brazilian School for Public Administration has traced the history of administrative reform efforts in Brazil and categorized them as holistic rather than gradual in the inclusiveness of their attempted change, prescriptive rather than suggestive in their language style, cognitive rather than valuational in their characterization of impediments to be overcome, and formal-legal rather than behavioral in their focus of action.[4] The reform efforts have been underlaid by that blend of pessimism and

[4] See Kleber Tatinge do Nascimento, *Change Strategy and Client System: Administrative Reform in Brazil* (Los Angeles: The School of Public Administration, University of Southern California, June, 1966).

optimism that leads Brazilians to resolve: "Vamos comecar tudo de novo" ("let us begin everything again"). Albert Hirschman calls this "the motivation-outruns-understanding style of problem-solving," a style that includes "endlessly repeated calls for a full, integrated, definitive, and rapid solution to the difficulties that are being encountered."[5]

The numerous attempts at structural and functional changes in public administration have seldom gone beyond formal-legal formulas. Brazilian government is characterized by a perfidious formalism. Celso Furtado observed from bitter experience that "an administrative system, like the Brazilian in its present state, is affected with such inertia that it can transform into mere formalism any attempt at reorganization that is not very well conceived."[6] Kleber Nascimento tells, for example, how the formal distinction between a "functionary" and an "extranumerary" has undermined attempts to develop a true civil service.[7] The functionary earns by examination a position created by statute and is promoted along positions which form a career. The extranumerary is admitted by "proof of capability" to a "function" created by decree; he is not promotable but receives "salary increases along a series of functions." Such formal distinctions continually undermine attempts at serious reform.

The Improvised Solutions

Within the Brazilian public administration, advancement is earned through a process of grit and determination and *jeito*. "Dar um jeito" is to find a solution to a problem regardless of laws or other norms. Basically, *jeito* may spring from nothing more than the Brazilian instinct for survival in a formalistic world; it is a flexible and pragmatic approach to formally unsolvable problems. *Jeito* rejects the view that ascriptive or particularistic relations within the bureaucracy are necessarily corrupt or pathological.

5 Albert O. Hirschman, *Journeys Toward Progress* (New York: The Twentieth Century Fund, 1963), 238.

6 Furtado, *Perspectivas da Economia Brasileira* (Rio de Janeiro: Superior Institute for Brazilian Studies, 1958), 79.

7 Nascimento, *Change Strategy and Client System*, 431.

It embraces kinship ties and personal connections insofar as they can avoid bureaucratic red tape and bring about expeditious solutions. It is ironic that João Goulart's reform commission inveighed that "not a single act practiced by public servants is to result from improvisation, but from previous decisions, matured and articulated into plans."[8] By improvisation or *jeito* Brazilians overcome or, rather, outflank the formalism that might otherwise result in utter stagnation and frustration.

Jeito cannot be done away with by law; it is indeed a product of formal-legalism. Only by taking a more pragmatic and experimental approach to the entire reform and development of public administration will the incidence of, and necessity for, *jeito* be lowered. Government reformers have usually confronted public administration development as a problem more of prescription, organization, and classification than of research, education, and training. Vargas' Inter-Party Commission for Federal Administrative Reform in 1953 specifically excluded "a revolution in the psychology of the public servant" from the scope of its reform.[9] Castello Branco's commission originally urged that "a change of mentality" be considered among the several elements of its proposed reform, but its final proposal was overwhelmingly "instrumental" and "functional" rather than educational.

Conclusions

Brazilian public administration shares all of the stresses and strains of the transitional society of which it is a part. It is a morass of conflicting tendencies and unresolved tensions which result in strangulation and stagnation and some grudging innovation and development. Lack of much innovation may be due less to traditionalism in practice than to discontinuity in staff and program. There may be a discordance between the structure of the bureaucracy and the values of the bureaucrats on the one side and their behavior on the other. Like Brazilian society at large, the public administration is characterized by unevenness, by high points of effectiveness but also vast lacunae of wastefulness.

8 *Ibid.,* 222.
9 *Ibid.,* 251.

A great deal may still be accomplished by structural and functional reforms and reorganizations; what is really called for, however, is a graduated and flexible strategy. Honey's basic emphasis on the importance of empirical research, systematic knowledge, training and education, and technical advisory assistance offers a structural basis for public administration development. Particularly in its long-term considerations, Honey's approach is a departure from the recommendations of the various reform commissions since the 1930's. It deserves a sympathetic, critical hearing.

THE HONEY ESSAY

Its Political Premises

One of the underlying views of Honey's analysis is that "the most favorable condition for any nation is one in which the citizenry controls the selection of political leaders." Members of the government which currently rules Brazil may agree with this viewpoint as an ideal. They may also remonstrate that Brazil itself is far from being in optimum condition; that it is an underdeveloped country; that it is threatened by inflation, corruption, and "communism"; and that it needs a "strong" government. Such conditions are used by the "Revolution" to justify the *golpe* that brought it to power in April, 1964, and the sequence of Institutional Acts that suspended the political rights of "subversives," voided the multifarious political parties, declared the indirect election of the President, and invested the military courts with extraordinary powers.

Despite the open, compromising, peaceful nature of the Brazilian stereotype, Brazil would not be a true democracy even under "normal" conditions. Fundamental facts of the Brazilian political situation are that about 50 per cent of the country is illiterate and that illiterates are not allowed to vote. Brazil has a paucity of viable institutions capable of representing the interests of broadly based segments of the population. It lacks sufficient institutions to press for popular reforms and simultaneously regulate their demands. There are, for example, neither responsible political parties nor effective labor unions. The output side of the Brazilian government has probably developed beyond the input side; consequently it is difficult to articulate the "public interest." In times of crisis, the army is the arbiter, since it has the power to control conflict and regards itself as having the right, indeed the obligation, to do so. The legitimacy of the army comes from its self-image as a broadly based national institution. It sees itself therein as the true repository of Brazilian "democracy."

For public administration development, the significance of the divergency between Honey's idea of the "most favorable [political] condition" and the actual Brazilian situation is unclear. It is itself a subject for hypotheses and research. Does the military have a penchant for planning and the politician for muddling through? Where does the military's anti-corruption shade over into anti-"subversion"? How does its command structure balance against its reluctance to change? Can public administration development be left to the politicians? Can it be left to the military? To a great extent, these questions are merely academic. Brazilian public administration development must start from where Brazil finds itself now; differences between values and behavior, however, can be important for the direction and magnitude of change possible.

Getting Started

The problems of starting any program of the magnitude suggested by Honey are not to be underestimated. They relate to both technical and political difficulties and to the classical dilemma of development breaking out of vicious circles. The very conditions that make public administration underdeveloped tend to maintain its underdevelopment.

The Honey essay is supposedly addressed in the first instance to "the governmental leaders in Latin America." It is doubtful that the governmental leaders of Brazil, confronted by other immediate competing demands, feel that they have the time, patience, or training to read and digest the essay. A real problem is how to make the need for public administration felt as a more immediate demand by the government leaders and how to create the kinds of pressures for innovation and reform that they can understand. The fact that most Brazilian reform efforts have stopped at the legislative phase is ample demonstration of the need on the part of reformers for a strategy of breakthrough to get the job done. In the abstract, the establishment of a national council on the public service would seem an excellent starting point for the consideration and implementation of Honey's proposals. In fact, such councils or commissions, variously composed of political leaders and administrative technicians, have been used in the past without notable success. The Special Commission on Administrative Reform Studies (COMESTRA), created by presidential decree in October, 1964, was presided over by the Minister of Planning and composed of politicians, public administrators, military men, and businessmen. Its proposed reforms are the basis for legislation now before Congress. General Costa e Silva, as president, could convoke a new commission, but there is no guarantee that a new commission would be more receptive to Honey's proposals.

The problem of how to begin to translate Honey's approaches into action is not insuperable. Brazil has already implemented some of them in a typically uneven and unplanned fashion. Brazilian education in public administration is perhaps the most advanced in Latin America, and attempts are under way to expand and modernize programs in political science, sociology, economics, and anthropology. Although no research has yet been done in Brazil to compare with the systematic and comprehensive MIT-CENDES studies of the Venezuelan polity, a few Brazilians are beginning to examine their own political culture using modern social science techniques. They are doing research on federal and state administration, and they are planning centers to study urban and municipal governmental problems. Among the recommendations of COMESTRA are a Central Advisory Staff for High Level Administration and a complementary High Level Training Center.

In a country of the size and diversity of Brazil, there are many prospective points of initiative. Honey's ideas should be circulated generally among the various schools and departments of public administration, law, and the social sciences. They would actually have the most intellectual interest and practical appeal to these academic institutions. An immediate effect could be the expansion of their activities and programs. They might adopt some recommendations on their own initiative, and propose other measures with the assistance of governmental agencies and international or foreign organizations.

The biennial national meeting of representatives from the twenty or so public administration programs in Brazil might turn out to be as important a point of departure as a special commission. Selected professors from law and the social sciences might be asked to join in a central discussion of the essay or some variation of it, and a standing committee might be set up to implement and nationalize the recommendations of the biennial meeting. Another point of departure might simply be the Brazilian School of Public Administration (EBAP) at the Getúlio Vargas Foundation. EBAP has sufficient staff, structure, prestige, and perspective to assume a national position in public administration development.

The idea of looking for a single national council of the public service as the mainspring for an integrated strategy of public administration development may be impracticable. A representative council may not have the requisite political power and professional perspective. Important elements of reform and innovation may come from such commissions on the federal, regional, state, and local levels. But development in different areas may spring from various groups and combinations, including the governor, the opposition party, the military, the bureaucracy itself, the universities, and the users of public services. In Rio Grande do Sul, a prestigious State Council on the Public Service is chiefly responsible for the most advanced personnel administration in Brazil. In Bahia, the opposition party recently played a critical role in the passage of the governor's reform legislation. In Maranhão, the army might well represent the key group for administrative change. The technicians of administrative reform and development will have to be flexible enough to seek the wielders of power wherever they may be.

Information and Research

Attempts at change should ideally be based on a comprehensive knowledge of existing information, but there is no single recognized source in Brazil of material on Brazilian government and public administration. The EBAP library, while modest, is undoubtedly the best collection, and it would probably offer the best prospect for the establishment of a general documentation center. More specialized libraries might be located at other schools and centers according to their scholarly emphases. For example, Brazilian politics might be assigned to the Department of Political Science at the Federal University of Minas Gerais; social studies, to the Faculty of Philosophy at the State University of São Paulo; urban government, to the Brazilian Institute for Municipal Administration (IBAM); and so on.

In each case, the institutions would already have basic libraries in their appointed areas, but they would probably have developed in an ad hoc way. The attempt to establish systematic and exhaustive collections will demand new injections of money, personnel, and purpose. Such plans call not only for expanded library purchases and more auxiliary equipment but also for basic bibliographical studies, improved library science programs, and increased usage of libraries. Several U.S. centers of Latin American studies are assiduously gathering libraries on Brazilian politics and society, and they have the resources to acquire private Brazilian collections wholesale. Measures should be taken to see that the richer U.S. institutions share more of their knowledge and techniques and that they leave copies of original works in Brazil.

The *Bibliografía Brasileira de Administracão Pública* lists about 7,000 items published in Brazil between 1940 and 1961, and the *Bibliografía Brasileira de Ciências Sociais* lists approximately 12,000 between 1954 and 1960.[10] But most Brazilian studies related to public administration can be categorized in three basic approaches corresponding to three successive phases of public administration in Brazil: the juridical, the technical, and the sociological.[11] The beginning of a new phase has not meant the discontinuing of older approaches, but rather their joining together with a shifting emphasis toward a newer approach.

[10] See Ivan L. Richardson, *Bibliografía Brasileira de Administracão Pública* (Rio de Janeiro: Getúlio Vargas Foundation, 1964); and *Bibliografía Brasileira de Ciências Sociais* (Rio de Janeiro: Brazilian Institute of Bibliography and Documentation, 1954–60).
[11] See Peter D. Bell, "Political Science: Public Administration and Development," *Brazil: Field Research Guide in the Social Sciences* (New York: Columbia University, 1966).

The juridical approach is the most venerable and persistent. It is distinguished by its attempt to find legalistic solutions—most often on the basis of abstract theory—to Brazilian administrative problems. Even today Brazilian literature on public administration is rich in formal-legal description and analysis and constitutional and legal theory. There is, for example, a plethora of material on the rights and obligations of public functionaries. This almost exclusively juridical approach to problems of public administration until the mid-1930's reinforced the behavioral formalism that enshrouded the real problems and that was itself an obstacle to their solution.

The technical approach is characterized by the search for universal rules for public administration and the promotion of "how-to-do-it" techniques that were derived not from Brazilian experience but from the scientific school abroad. The technicians insisted that there was one best way of achieving efficiency in administration and assumed that the greater rationalization of North American and European societies had given their public administrators special insight into that way. They confused the conditions of development in the United States and Europe with the preconditions for development in Brazil. It is ironic that U.S. students of public administration have given increasing importance to behavioral and attitudinal description and analysis, whereas the Brazilians have until recently clung to the technical prescriptions derived from the earlier U.S. literature.

As long as the juridical and technical approaches prevailed, the social and political environment of public administration received little attention except as a corrupting factor to be excluded. Both approaches rested in part on conceptions of public administration that were distinctly neutral politically and socially. The sociological approach grew out of a recognition that the failures at reform in the 1930's and 1940's were due to the failure to relate the new techniques to the Brazilian social and political context. The Brazilian sociologists have been interested in the network of social values that underlie administrative behavior and hence impede or facilitate administrative innovation and development. They have been particularly influenced by the Weberian and Parsonian pattern variables as analytical instruments of public administration development, but most of this literature is still written on a theoretical and holistic plane and drawn principally from foreign models.

Within the economic research centers of the Ministry of Planning and the Vargas Foundation calculated attempts are being made to meet some of the information deficiencies related to economic development, but no systematic effort has been made to map out the research needs related to political development for Brazil. Little basic statistical and descriptive material exists on the Brazilian government. When the Institute of Public Service in Bahia set out to collect such data as a basis for their state reform program, they found that it took months to uncover the legislation that established some government agencies or to find the number of active employees in the government. A good deal of information that would be helpful for the more effective operation of the government is unknown or forgotten. Some rather basic data gathering and revealing of simple facts might in itself improve public administration or at least suggest measures for its improvement. Such work could often be done within the government on a self-study basis. For example, a recent descriptive study of the structure and activities of the personal staff of the President prompted its author, the *sub-chefe* of the Gabinete Civil, to submit several suggestions for reform of the office.[12] The DASP is conducting a census of the federal government which should assist planners and reformers.

Fundamental research on the government and the citizen, which might provide a basis for long-term action and education reforms, is still relatively unfamiliar and even suspect in Brazil. Political studies have consisted of theories or ideas spun out of the minds of their authors or lifted bodily from foreign models, histories woven together with literary citations, exegeses on constitutions and laws, personal observations and reminiscences, and hybrids of these approaches. Such studies range from formal-legalism to neo-Marxism and from obscurant-mysticism to journalism. Leftists are apt to spurn a scientific approach to the polity that is non-Marxist; rightists resent the tendency of the social sciences to put the status quo in question. Both of them are apt to view the modern social sciences as products of North American

<hr/>

[12] See Luiz Navarro de Britto, "O Gabinete Civil (1965)" (Brasilia: Government of Brazil, 1966).

cultural "imperialism." They attribute both too little and too much power to survey questionnaires and consequently regard social scientists with disdain or suspicion.

The sociologists who have questioned the past assumptions about public administration development in Brazil have failed to follow through with empirical research. Relatively modest research on governmental functions needs to be done before responding to such basic questions as the extent to which the bureaucracy can become an effective instrument of economic change without taking on the complex set of characteristics implied by an application of Weberian ideal types. It may be that the bureaucracy in Brazil should adapt to structures and values that are less characteristic of Weberian than of transitional societies. Moreover, the sociologists have failed to focus rigorously and narrowly on the expressly political aspects of administrative change and their implications for changes in the structure or allocation of power in the society. In the United States, such a focus would be the responsibility of the political scientist.

Even where Brazilian professors are inclined toward modern social sciences and empirical research, they often lack the full-time academic positions, the requisite training, the auxiliary equipment, and the intellectual and political environment in which to pursue their research interests. Some state-level studies have been done on voting behavior and political parties: A study of the social background of Guanabara state legislators was undertaken; several community power studies, particularly in Minas Gerais, have been completed; and industrial sociology and urban migration have been studied in São Paulo. The Department of Political Science at Minas Gerais is currently working on a research survey of the political culture of Belo Horizonte and plans to expand it by stages to other parts of Minas Gerais and then to other regions of Brazil. Until now, however, most of the research has been spotty rather than systematic, and little has been done in any comprehensive way to show how the Brazilian government functions or how citizens relate to it.

The approximately one hundred North American graduate students and professors who are now doing field studies in Brazil undoubtedly outnumber the Brazilians who are working full time in social science research. From a Brazilian perspective, the North

American studies often have only marginal relevance to Brazilian development. North American researchers can contribute to the body of knowledge on Brazilian society, but American researchers cannot fully answer Brazilian research needs. The real problem is to see that Brazilians have the training and support to do important research themselves and to join in truly collaborative efforts.

Empirical research is not a substitute for original and creative thought, and the one should not be stressed to the exclusion of the other, but Brazil already has a number of social philosophers who think holistically but abstractly about their country. The work of social scientists will become the basis for action, and in that sense creative, when their theory becomes more manageable and their research more concrete. What is needed now are studies which seek to describe and explain socio-political institutions and processes through positing testable hypotheses and applying systematic empirical research, identifying regularities in behavior, seeking quantification of data, and discovering explanatory concepts and values. The broadest and simplest goal of the development of social science research as such is to reveal and explain Brazilian social reality; the social sciences in Brazil must be used not only for general description and explanation but also for narrower identification and analysis of developmental problems and suggestion for alternative solutions. Social thought will inevitably become less elegant, but effective social action, including public administration improvement, may become more feasible.

Education and Training

As long as particularistic and ascriptive criteria are used to select and promote public administrators, who are poorly paid at that, Brazilians will have little incentive to improve their education and training for the public service. The assumption here is that the complex needs of this industrializing society will make themselves felt in new demands for governmental effectiveness and that the country will see fit to support the new standards with appropriate salaries and status. High technical standards of effectiveness have already been achieved in some critical areas of the present government such as the National Bank for Economic Development (BNDE), the Ministry of Planning, and sectors of the Ministry of Finance; the supporting salaries, however, have been bolstered by a combination of *jeito* and special government contracts, supplements from AID and other international agencies, and intragovernmental personnel loans. The present elite of economists in the government, as the administrative elite under the Vargas government, is not secured by the administrative system; it exists because of extraordinary political support by the Castello Branco and Costa e Silva governments.

Prospective training and education measures vary from relatively short-range programs like executive conferences, management internships, and in-service training to long-range concerns like improved training in public affairs and the social sciences, civic education, and the development of political leadership. The short-range programs could probably be implemented with the present resources of the government. But even the formalistic interpretation of the prevalent "merit system" stresses the entrance examinations rather than criteria for promotion, and consequently reduces the potential importance of in-service training. What is needed is the means to expand such training and to motivate public servants to take advantage of it. Intensive courses for in-service training are already offered at several levels in some areas of government and in cooperation with the various school and university programs. Since 1952 nearly 3,000 government employees have taken extension courses at EBAP; since 1957 IBAM has offered intensive courses to some 3,200 municipal administrators, including mayors and council presidents; DASP, the Institute of Public Service in Bahia, the School of Administration in Ceará, and the Institute of Administration of Rio Grande do Sul also sponsor in-service training activities.

Over a period of years, qualitative improvement in the public administration will have to be based in part on general changes in training in the social sciences and in education for public affairs and citizenship. Aside from the School of War, which functions somewhat analogously to the U.S. War College, and the Rio Branco Institute, which trains a foreign service elite quite expertly in old-fashioned diplomacy, Brazil today does not have a single school or academic program which is explicitly concerned with broadly conceived public and international affairs. The faculties of law have abstracted themselves from public affairs, even though they continue to be considered de facto schools of public affairs. The schools of public administration that have broken away from the faculties of law or evolved from in-service training programs are still characterized by juridical and technical approaches. The departments of social sciences, with few exceptions, tend to be juridical and theoretical in approach and to be lacking in empirically based behavioral and structural studies of Brazilian society.

According to the Anuários Estatísticos do Brasil, 30,974, or 21 per cent, of the 142,974 Brazilian students who entered the universities in 1964, matriculated in sixty-one faculties of law. The law students represent a rising number and declining but still large percentage of university students in Brazil. With the exception of the faculties of philosophy, which are nearly colleges in themselves, the law schools remain the largest faculties in Brazil. Brazil in 1963 had sixty law faculties, with 1,746 professors and 28,534 students; eighty-nine economics (mainly accounting) faculties, with 1,908 professors and 12,739 students; fourteen administration (both public and business) courses, with 288 professors and 1,719 students; and nine sociology and politics courses, with 142 professors and 633 students. Numerically, the dominance of law over public administration and the social sciences is overwhelming, and the influence is even greater when it is considered that most professors were probably trained in law.

Faculties of law in Brazil are traditionally the schools of the Brazilian governing elite, and the experience of the law faculties inevitably influences the character of the government. The nineteenth-century academies of law were considered "the anterooms of Parliament." But legal education in Brazil has not kept abreast of changes in Brazilian society; in the twentieth century, the contribution of law graduates to social change has been marginal at best. Law is regarded as an instrument of the status quo rather than development, and the lawyer is not so much sought out as circumvented by initiators of change and administrators of reform. Much of the recent important legislation in Brazil—for example, the Agrarian Reform, Banking Reform, Tax Reform, and Capital Markets laws—was drafted by economists rather than by lawyers. The *fazendeiro-advogado,* or farmer-lawyer, mentality that ruled traditional Brazilian society is not capable of the legislative or administrative innovation demanded for Brazilian development today.

Brazilian legal education is oriented toward a systematic knowledge of black-letter law. Professors deliver their lectures in the elegant but abstruse expository style of Coimbra, the ancient Portuguese university where Brazilians studied law until their independence. Lawyers typically look to professorships in law schools to cap the prestige they have won in private practice and public office. The students, who also have jobs outside the universities, hurriedly and distractedly attend lectures. At the end of the academic year, they cram for final examinations by memorizing abstracts from poorly compiled course readers. Law graduates are considered "cultured" by virtue of having attended faculties of law, but fewer than 20 per cent of them ever practice law.

The paradox that characterizes the faculties of law is a widespread phenomenon in Brazil: what from the outside appear to be highly rigid institutions are, when viewed from the inside, entirely lacking in institutional solidity. The problem may not be vested interests in the maintenance of the faculties as they are, but lack of any vested institutional interests at all. These apparent bastions of conservatism are more nearly shimmering mirages with their comings and goings of professors and students. The "traditionalism" of the faculties may in fact be owed as much to default as to purpose. The professors and students rushing to and from their classes and jobs do not have the time, energy, or other resources to contemplate needs or reforms in approach and curriculum. Their struggle is not for change but to keep up with what they are doing.

The social sciences in Brazil originated in the law schools, because of recognition of the public nature of the law graduate's role in society. Over the last twenty-five years, the establishment of new faculties of philosophy and economic sciences has been accompanied by divestment of the social sciences by faculties of law. The compartmentalized structure of Brazilian universities isolates faculties of law from the new economics and newer political science, sociology, and psychology. Where law still dominates the social sciences, its formal techniques impede development of the behavioral approach that law itself needs. Brazilian legal education has become separated not only from the modern social sciences but also from present-day social reality. Legal education in Brazil may now be comparable to that in the United States in 1935, when one American observed that it was "so inadequate, wasteful, blind and foul that it will take twenty years of unremitting effort to make it half-way equal to its job.[13] Before law can be transformed into an instrument for development, legal education will need to be put in a social context, and faculties of law will have to be changed in content, approach, and structure.

It would be a mistake to underestimate the power of one of Brazil's oldest, largest, most prestigious, most traditional, and most elusive educational institutions to resist radical reform; however, changes are occurring in legal education which may eventually have important accumulative effect. Recent innovations include the introduction of special postgraduate courses to explain the new economic legislation to practicing lawyers; the requirement of legal internships for advanced law students, and the development of a government intern program by the state of Guanabara; the establishment of a minimum law curriculum by the Federal Law of Directives and Bases; the extension of university legal assistance into urban slums, as in Rio de Janeiro and São Paulo, and into interior towns, as in Ceará; and the creation of the Center for Study and Research in Legal Education (CEPED) at the State University of Guanabara. Assisted by AID and the Ford Foundation, CEPED is experimenting with new teaching and research methods and is particularly trying to break down the nice categories of the traditional abstract system, to relate legal studies to the social sciences, and to focus them on real development problems. But widespread implementation of the CEPED experience in the law schools would presume such formidable changes as the renovation of the *catedrático* (proprietary professorship) system, the conversion of the *bacharel* mentality, and the interpenetration of heretofore separate faculties.

The integration of public administration and the modern social sciences is no less required than the integration of law and the behavioral sciences. Both the juridical and technical approaches

[13] Cited from Karl Llewellyn, "On What Is Wrong with So-Called Legal Education" (35 *Columbia Law Review* 651), in "Note: Modern Trends in Legal Education" (64 *Columbia Law Review* 710).

need to be tempered by a greater understanding of Brazilian social reality. The EBAP curriculum, by virtue of the school's size, location, age, and prestige, serves as a model for Brazil; and its course titles would seem to indicate the school's belief in a social science foundation to public administration. In fact, until recently, EBAP did not have a single sociological or political empiricist on its staff, and its extensive research and publications program has yet to produce any systematic empirical studies aside from a few cases. A six-year AID agreement that included visiting professors and graduate fellowhips between the University of Southern California and EBAP, Bahia, and Rio Grande do Sul must take credit for much of the strength in public administration techniques at the Brazilian schools; it must also bear some responsibility for their weakness in the modern social sciences.

The development of the social sciences ought to be fundamental to the training for public affairs, including public administration. But separate courses in sociology and politics are attended by only 5 per cent of Brazilian university students and given by a comparable number of professors. Some tradition of sociology at least exists in São Paulo, Rio de Janeiro, Belo Horizonte, Recife, and Porto Alegre; but political science, beyond the chairs of the General Theory of the State in the law faculties and their extension into social science courses, is at an incipient stage. Brazil has just one doctorate in political science.

The recently established Department of Political Science at Minas Gerais brought elements of political science from three faculties into what will become the first department within a Central Institute of the Human Sciences and represents an initial attempt to develop an empirical approach to the study of politics in Brazil. The Department is being assisted by a Ford Foundation grant to support graduate study abroad of prospective Brazilian professors in the Department, to bring visiting professors, lecturers, and consultants to the Department, to sponsor national meetings of political scientists, to execute empirical research projects, and to build a strong basic library in political science.

Other projects of the Minas type, including restructuring of Brazilian resources and contributions from abroad, will have to be undertaken to build up centers of social science strength at various points in the country and to link them in collaborative research and in the exchange of teaching materials and personnel. In most cases, the contributions will be from the United States because that country is most advanced in the empirical approach to the social sciences; but efforts should also be made to solicit assistance from England, France, Germany, and Italy.

The development of political leadership and of an informed citizenry is a wider and more subtle problem. The tendency toward reorganization of the universities from separate faculties into central institutes may eventually result in basic studies programs that would give professionals in all fields some education in the social sciences. Student politics have long been a training ground for Brazilian political leaders; however, the 1964 Revolution has banished the old student organizations by decree (and consequently sent them underground) and attempted to confine the new organizations to "student business." The distrust between the government and the university students is more a generational than ideological problem. But it has certainly influenced the government's education policy, and it may be having profound effects on the political attitudes of the new generation, which cannot be ignored, if only because more than 50 per cent of Brazilians are now under twenty. The present limited military dictatorship at times seems more concerned with "eliminating" politics than developing politicians.

An underlying need of political development is to bring the curricula and concerns of the schools nearer to Brazilian reality and to relate them to problems of development. Law and public administration should be integrated with the social sciences, but the social sciences themselves are badly in need of modernization. A more systematic empirical approach to political, legal, and administrative studies might expedite change by identifying leverage points and making the efforts of reformers more efficient. Among public administrators, politicians, and citizens at large, better knowledge of Brazilian reality might effect more realistic expectations and more certain achievements in attempts at development. Thus political development may in the long run be importantly tied to social science development, which is in turn tied to a series of structural, financial, and attitudinal problems.

Conclusions

The Honey essay offers a series of suggestions for public administration development that seem good in the abstract and that are feasible in varying degrees. Some of the ideas are limited by the political situation, and others are affected by the scarcity of resources or the strength of prevailing traditions.

The Brazilian government for now is more concerned about the efficiency of its public administration than about extending political participation. It is more immediately interested in the training of economic and administrative technicians than in basic education in the social sciences, in public affairs, or even for active citizenship. The consequence may be promising for some of the shorter term measures that can be executed primarily out of present resources and for longer term measures that are specifically related to economic planning. In some cases, the extraordinary executive powers of the government may allow it to forego the politically popular for the "technically right"; but the discrepancy between the words and action of the Castello Branco government in relation to reform of the public administration was an impressive testimony to the bureaucracy's resistance to change.

The government has recently shown awareness of the need for reform of its university system, but it remains to be seen whether the basic structural reforms called for can be effected. It is doubtful that the government will explicitly relate university reforms to political development or even to the development of its public administration and that it will actively promote the modernization and expansion of the social sciences in the universities. But changes in approach to the long-run development of the public administration can still occur through a combination of local initiative, government response, and outside assistance.

Chile

RICHARD A. FEHNEL

INTRODUCTION

The application of Professor Honey's thesis can lead to an elaborate analysis. In the case of Chile we have addressed our attention to the political system, which for our purposes can be seen as having three aspects: the process of political socialization wherein members of society encounter institutions which form attitudes and expectations regarding the political system, and which develop capabilities and qualities enabling people to participate in the system; the status of political competition, which provides an array of institutions acting as filtration and coalescence points for disparate special interests of the citizenry; and the structure of political authority, which is responsible for legitimizing public interests and operationalizing them in action programs.

Following the discussions of each of these aspects, an attempt is made to point out operational considerations which may affect the development of reform strategy in the area under consideration and to call attention to proposals which may be considered.[1]

POLITICAL SOCIALIZATION

Chile's political society is composed of a mosaic of institutions in which every Chilean has been involved to some degree: families,

[1] Acknowledgment is hereby made to the large number of Chilean government officials, educators, politicians, and "interested citizens" whose patience and cooperation made this report possible; to Bruce Gibb of the Ford Foundation, Santiago, Chile, whose intellectual and logistic support were crucial; and to the Graduate School of Business and Public Administration, Cornell University, whose Latin American Internship Program, under the guidance of Dean William Carmichael, made it possible for me to be in Chile for some eighteen months.

educational institutions, churches, and social and work groups. All have the common element of influencing attitudes about political figures and institutions, thus affecting desires to engage in political competition and influencing the ability to work co-operatively and equitably with others.

Preschool Experience and the Socialization Processes

The importance of education in the formative years has long been recognized. The processes by which a child learns remains a fertile ground for research, but there is agreement that informal learning in the home sets patterns for lifelong adherence to selected values and attitudes.

Although no studies have been conducted to determine precisely what values are stressed by Chilean parents, available statistical data suggest that the circumstances of environment are not conducive to the development of positive attitudes with respect to responsible citizenship. The 1960 Chilean census indicates that there are some 270,000 families which either lack one of the parents (because of death, separation, or annulment) or are held together by a common-law marriage. The same census shows that 80 per cent of the population is housed in dwellings described as "in need of major repairs of walls or structural elements" or "unrepairable." For the rural areas, this figure exceeds 90 per cent of the population.

According to the 1960 census, the economic situation of most Chilean families is depressed. Only 32 per cent of the population over the age of 12 is economically active. The agricultural sector has the lowest percentage, 28 per cent, with an estimated average annual income of about $280 per worker (U.S. dollars).

Given unstable family conditions, poor housing, and low incomes, the paramount concern of many Chilean families is with the day-to-day struggle for existence, while the concern for developing a positive civic ethic within the child has an understandably low priority.

In the middle- and the upper-class families the environment for promoting positive attitudes toward the political system is undoubtedly better. However, the middle-class Chilean has consumption tastes that outstrip his economic resources, resulting in an unbalanced concern for personal economic gain. In a traditional society, such as Chile's, this concern does not sublimate into a popular program for action at the national or even at the community level. Rather it seeks resolution at the personal or family level. Family customs and national economic problems aggravate the situation. A constant inflationary situation encourages immediate gratification rather than saving for future satisfaction. In the parent-child relationship there is a tendency for parents to be indulgent to the limit of their economic capacity and to rely on servants for many aspects of child rearing.

How does this affect political socialization? The child does not learn discipline from the parent; he expects immediate gratification. He has no authority figure which consistently requires compliance. His parents, with tastes that outrun their resources, frequently engage in economic shortcuts such as falsifying tax returns, avoiding the payment of assessments until inflation has diminished the amount owed, holding two or three jobs without being concerned about effective performance, etc. The state is something to be outwitted because "everyone does it." The government is not to be trusted, they say, because it is staffed by political appointees who are out to serve themselves and their friends.

As preparation for formal education, the home, particularly in rural areas, leaves much to be desired. According to the 1960 census, for example, in rural areas 39 per cent of the population over the age of 25 never attended school and 32 per cent had three years or less of primary education: Can there, then, be much parental concern for preparing children for school? The same census indicates that 85 per cent of rural area children between the ages of 5 and 9 have never received any instruction.

While little is being done directly to improve the home environment of the child, steps are being undertaken to integrate the adult into modern society with hoped-for side benefits for the child.

The Public Education System and Socialization

Positive attitudes and skills with respect to the political system could conceivably be generated in courses and activities in grades one through six in the primary school. A social science methodologist advising a Ministry of Education curriculum improvement project in Chile has reported that aside from courses dealing with various aspects of Chilean history, and those requiring rote memorization of names and places, little social science instruction related to the political system is offered in these grades. Some information is provided with respect to symbols such as the flag and basic documents like the constitution. Current affairs of any type are not discussed in the classroom.

The significant political socializing role of the educational system, however, is not directly measurable in the content of civic courses in the curriculum. It is measurable instead in the quality and quantity of the total output of the system. The focus of the educational stream in the past has been to prepare students intellectually for entrance to the universities. Vocational preparation for the vast majority of students not expecting to attend universities was not given much attention. It is not surprising therefore to find an alarming drop-out rate in school attendance. A 1966 publication by the Ministry of Education shows that only 11 per cent of the children in the appropriate age group are enrolled in the last year of secondary school, and only 68 per cent of the children of the appropriate age group are enrolled in the sixth grade.[2]

Since 1964, educational reform has been a major concern in Chile. The Ministry of Education, with assistance from the Ford Foundation, has undertaken major programs of teacher training and curriculum revision. Improved subject matter and methodological approaches to teaching mathematics, science, languages, and the social sciences are being stressed. An entire year has been added to the primary education curriculum, and plans for expansion of vocational education at the secondary level are under way.

University Education and Socialization

Current approaches in university education with regard to the political socialization processes indicate that the university has a

[2] Ministerio de Educación Pública, *Cuadernos de la Superintendencia,* "La Reforma Educacional Chilena y sus Proyecciones." Santiago, Chile, Sept., 1966, p. 46.

limited awareness of its responsibility in this area. Faculties continue to ponder the great philosophical questions of the respective disciplines or professions, while the important social questions of the Chilean present often go unasked.

The most encouraging evidence of concern with such questions is found in summer construction projects conducted by university students. Each summer a few students go into the social and economic backwaters to build schools and community centers. Until recently the universities, as institutions, have played a negligible role in this endeavor. Financial support comes mainly from the Ministry of Education, coordination from the office of the Presidential Youth Adviser, and leadership from the students and from technicians hired out of the building trades.

The university student has ample opportunity to participate in the university political parties, which are closely connected to the national parties. Here he learns party loyalty and earns party favors. However, political party activity is not normally characterized by objective, long-range approaches to socio-economic issues, and the academic milieu does not offset partisan "socialization." The net result is that the politically "socialized" student is conditioned in a subjective, political "pressure cooker."

In order to generate countervailing influences, major changes must occur in the information and knowledge upon which university courses are developed. This, of course, implies departure from the historical and metaphysical approaches and increased attention to pragmatic and empirical research. Such changes, which cannot be made easily, involve the development of investigative skills and a stress on objectivity. It will be necessary to learn such tools as statistics and social psychology.

One recent development is that a National Research Commission has been established as a sub-agency of the Council of University Rectors. This Commission will orient, promote, plan, and coordinate the development of research priorities, taking into account national developmental needs. Its Board of Directors is composed of twenty-eight members from the university, the government, and the private sector. While it is an important step in the direction of increasing university research, and in attempting to coordinate research goals with national needs, the ability of this group to work with faculties of the universities in the distribution of research resources is unknown.

*University-Professional Education for Careers in
Public Administration*

The role of the universities in preparing professionals for the public service is, of course, of special interest. The term "professionals" is meant to include administrative as well as functional specialists such as lawyers, engineers, doctors, or economists employed by the government. Training administrative specialists is done primarily in the School of Political and Administrative Sciences of the Law Faculty of the University of Chile, and in the School of Economics and the Institute of Administration (INSORA) of the Faculty of Economic Sciences of the same University.

The program of studies in the School of Political and Administrative Sciences[3] is aimed at producing five different types of specialists: foreign service officers, customs officials, social welfare administrators, financial administrators, and general administrators. The rate of turnover in the government is so slow in some of these areas that less than 10 per cent of the graduates find work in their specialties. The director of the school reports that out of six hundred entering students in a school year fewer than seventy will finish their studies.

Both faculties indicate a desire to prepare students for top positions in administration, but neither has been able to analyze and incorporate in their curricula the knowledge and experience needed to perform adequately in such positions. The Ministry of Education hired the top three graduates of the School of Political and Administrative Sciences for four consecutive years. It has now abandoned the practice because it found the students were not in fact prepared for administrative jobs. Part of the problem is also a tacit recognition that in Chile government professional positions tend to be ascribed rather than achieved.

Teaching methods in these schools are typical of the methods used in most university classrooms. The primary method of instruction is the lecture, which is built upon philosophical conceptualization spiced with anecdotes from personal experience. The role of the student is passive; generally classes are so large that the possibility of much student participation is ruled out.

[3] It is not possible to specialize in political science. Of the twenty-five courses available only five can loosely be called political science courses.

Part-time instructors have little opportunity or incentive to spend time with students. In the School of Economics, of the thirty-two instructors giving classes in administration, three devote all of their time to teaching; an additional nine earn a full salary doing research to supplement their teaching. The rest are persons who spend much of their time in occupations not directly related to teaching activities; four are on the University payroll in administrative positions, and the others are paid by the hour for their classroom services but, in accordance with University policy, receive no pay for time spent in preparation of classes, correcting exams, or counseling students.

INSORA is frequently thought of as the research arm of the Faculty for administration, but it also has a graduate training program in administration (Programa de Administración para Graduados). Of the instructors in this program, five spend full time on teaching and research and six are part-time hourly instructors. The dean of the Faculty of Economic Sciences is aggressively trying to reverse the part-time/full-time ratio through a comprehensive five-year development plan aimed at having 85 per cent of all courses taught by full-time faculty.

The School of Political and Administrative Sciences of the Law Faculty and the Customs School in Valparaiso, which is part of this School, use large numbers of part-time instructors. The curricula of these institutions is highly legalistic. As with most professional schools in the universities of Chile, we find in these two faculties courses stressing the stereotyped traditional subject matter. The law courses emphasize legalistic aspects of administration and correct legal forms of administrative procedures. In the Economics Faculty the stress is more on organization and management. The student is taught procedural rationality and is offered little with respect to the basic reasons for government and its need to be responsive to the changing needs of society.

Universities in Latin America have been slow to pursue empirical research; the University of Chile is no exception. Research in public administration is particularly limited. In the Law Faculty the primary research organization is the Institute of Political and Administrative Sciences. It receives approximately 5 per cent of the budget appropriations of this faculty, and its staff is comprised of six persons who work two hours daily. They are not trained in empirical research techniques. The research and teaching are institutionally separated, and no mechanism exists to bring them together. Three of the Institute's staff are among the fifty-four part-time instructors in the School of Political and Administrative Sciences, but this is the only "overlap." Student research papers, almost entirely of a bibliographical nature, are not coordinated with the research activities of the Institute. The possibility of using students from the School as researchers in the Institute has not been explored.

Until very recently many of the same comments could be made of research at INSORA. In both business and public administration, INSORA was essentially a consulting organization. Although it accounted for as much as 38 per cent of the faculty budget, most of its funds were self-generated through consulting work. A conscious effort to channel consulting experience into the academic program was not made. Changes began, however, when staff members were sent abroad to study and returned with an awareness that they knew very little of Chilean governmental reality. A shift in policy has now occurred, and INSORA is commited to a program of empirical investigation.

At the undergraduate level, in the Faculty of Economic Sciences the separation between research and education also is characteristic. This is changing, however, in the face of recent reforms creating coordinating committees between research and teaching personnel, on a subject-matter basis.

There is incipient awareness of the potential of utilizing students in research, though this potential has not been seriously developed. Priority is being given to the development of the skills of staff members, principally through sending them abroad or through importing researchers to collaborate in domestic investigations.

In summary, to the present the university-trained public administrator has received theoretical, classroom preparation. Neither he nor the majority of his instructors have researched and analyzed the real world of public administration. He may be able to quote the legal and procedural requirements for a budget, but it is unlikely that he will be able to plan, program, or execute a budget which is tied to long-range development needs.

Technical training in public administration is also offered in the regional colleges. Six of the University of Chile's regional colleges offer a *tecnico* program of five semesters' duration. Classes are held in the evening since most of the enrolled students are full-time employees. The program is operated by the School of Political and Administrative Science, using part-time faculty members. A total of 615 persons were enrolled during 1966.

With respect to the preparation of specialists, such as lawyers, doctors, engineers, nurses, etc., who work in the public sector, many governmental officials express concern with the inadequate training in light of the functions to be performed. The extent of professional involvement in the government may be seen in Tables 1 and 2 below. Some attempt is made to update knowledge through postgraduate short courses. The pattern of postgraduate and improvement courses offered by the University of Chile is shown in Table 3.

It is not uncommon for specialists to achieve important decision-making posts in the government. Their ignorance of governmental and administrative affairs results in poorly conceived plans and in difficulties with managing budget and manpower resources as well as with organizational and procedural matters. Research into the means of improving the administrative capabilities of such professionals has not been undertaken. Instructors in the postgraduate and improvement courses are generally not administrative experts but specialists who have had some administrative experience.

Socialization and the Non-Integrated Adult

The main thrust of governmental efforts toward political socialization has been directed to that large group of adults who have not yet been integrated into the social, economic, and political life of Chile. While a full report of the myriad of programs undertaken by all sectors of the government is not possible, various programs of the Ministry of Education are noted by way of illustration.

The Ministry's programs in adult education can be divided into two main areas: regular education for adults who have not been able to continue their formal schooling, and the Programa Extraordinario de Educación Adulta. The regular education program has been in existence for many years, but the Frei administration

TABLE 1
DISTRIBUTION OF SELECTED PROFESSIONALS BY MINISTRIES

PROFESSION	Interior	Foreign Relations	Economy	Finance	Education	Justice	Public Works	Agriculture	Lands and Colonization	Labor and Social Security	Health	Mines	Total
Architects	2	—	8	20	11	1	278	1	—	5	31	—	357
Agricultural engineers	—	—	70	27	11	—	5	404	16	—	1	—	534
Civil engineers	7	—	72	4	13	—	272	1	2	2	15	28	416
Commercial engineers	1	—	68	25	7	—	2	5	—	—	1	3	112
Accountants	19	5	141	51	43	22	95	23	10	132	174	—	715
Physicians*	207	—	4	1	26	61	3	—	—	6	—	—	308
Nurses	16	—	2	—	100	1	—	—	1	5	1,244	—	1,368
Teachers*	5	—	—	—	8,178	1	56	16	1	—	182	—	8,439
Pub. adm.	110	169	35	65	19	18	6	4	2	8	1	2	439
Social workers	66	—	13	7	63	38	105	—	—	57	557	22	928
Physical technicians†	55	2	90	47	423	—	1,002	18	13	10	113	94	1,867

Source: Instituto de Administración, *Recursos Humanos de la Administración Pública Chilena, Informe Complementario; Clasificación Ocupacional* (Santiago de Chile, 1965), 67.

* Does not include those persons who are contracted by the hour.

† Have specialized training, but do not hold an engineering degree.

TABLE 2
DISTRIBUTION OF SELECTED PROFESSIONALS BY SECTOR OF EMPLOYMENT

Employment Sector	Total Number in Existence*	Public Sector	Private Sector	% Public Sector	% Private Sector
Architects	1,327	357	970	27.0	75.0
Dental surgeons	2,819	528	2,291	18.7	81.3
Agricultural engineers	1,495	534	961	35.7	64.3
Commercial engineers	845	112	733	13.3	86.7
Medical surgeons	4,809	3,317	1,482	69.2	30.8
Forestry engineers	55	2	53	3.6	96.4
Total:	11,350	4,850	6,490	42.8	57.2

Source: Instituto de Administración, *Recursos Humanos de la Administración Pública Chilena, Informe Complementario: Clasificación Ocupacional* (Santiago de Chile, 1965), 26.
* Estimated as of June, 1962.

has changed it so drastically that it is in essence new. Prior to this administration the same texts, the same teaching methods, and, indeed, the same classroom seats were used for the adults being trained as for children. Under the new system, there are evening and day classes in primary, secondary, and vocational

TABLE 3
NUMBER OF STUDENTS PER YEAR ENROLLED IN POSTGRADUATE
AND IMPROVEMENT COURSES BY SPONSORING SCHOOL
OF THE UNIVERSITY OF CHILE

SCHOOL	1962	1963	1964	1965	1966
Law	—	—	—	236	159
Medicine	—	—	220	88	534
Nursing	—	—	19	10	30
Health	79	85	—	—	142
Dental	—	—	27	111	61
Engineering	85	35	39	270	105
Educ. supervisors	—	—	—	—	82
Educ. counselors	—	—	—	—	105
Others	—	—	331	20	244
Total	164	120	636	735	1,462

Sources: Boletín Estadístico, Universidad de Chile, years 1962, 1963, and 1964. Informativo Estadístico, Universidad de Chile, years 1965 and 1966.

education in which the individual progresses according to his own ability. Texts are specially designed for adults, and instructors are trained in adult education, employing teaching techniques compatible with adult learning experiences.

The Programa Extraordinario de Educación Adulta is an entirely new activity. It is composed of two main parts: a literacy program and a community education program. The emphasis placed on this effort can be seen in the growth of its budget; in 1964 approximately 3.5 million escudos were budgeted; in 1965, 6.5 millions; and in 1966, approximately 13.2 millions. In 1966 and 1967 the literacy program was scheduled to give training to an estimated 300,000 persons, using a highly successful training technique developed in Brazil.

The community education program is built around community centers, one thousand of which have been opened in the past two years. The focus is on training in manual skills, for both men and women. The program is coordinated with courses given through the Instituto de Desarrollo Communitario (INDECO), which, while nominally independent of the Ministry of Education, receives financial and technical support from it. The basic purpose of INDECO is to teach self-sufficiency in a culture which has been dependent upon the *patron.*

The recognition of the need to provide political socialization to the marginal populations has been growing, and in the presidential election of 1964 it was made the center plank of the victorious Christian Democratic candidate's platform. The progress and scope of the swelling tide of activities can be seen in the following tables. Table 4 is a listing, by provinces, of the community organizations legally in existence as of June, 1966. Table 5 shows the number of new organizations created during succeeding time periods in a sample taken from data on four provinces.

In short, it can be seen that the political socialization processes for the "non-integrated" adult are active. Their effectiveness may perhaps be inferred from a comparison of election figures in the campaigns for House of Deputies in 1961 and 1965. In 1961, a total of 1,385,676 votes were cast. In 1965, 2,202,443 votes were cast. In 1961 the candidates of the large traditional, right-of-center parties received 51 per cent of the vote, while the large

TABLE 4

NUMBER OF EXISTING COMMUNITY ORGANIZATIONS, BY PROVINCE*

Province	J.V.	C.M.	C.D.	O.J.	C.C.A.
Tarapacá	83	119	135	9	11
Antofagasta	68	145	184	7	9
Atacama	47	68	96	8	13
Coquimbo	35	48	70	5	6
Aconcagua	66	118	125	12	11
Valparaíso	110	194	206	18	16
Santiago	820	1,500	2,300	120	132
O'Higgins	72	102	196	14	8
Colchagau	120	148	206	12	18
Curicó	40	110	142	8	12
Talca	58	94	109	9	13
Linares	43	108	133	6	5
Maule	36	51	86	7	11
Nuble	38	92	115	8	6
Concepción	169	209	333	10	29
Arauco	46	95	125	12	13
Bío Bío	31	54	86	2	4
Malleco	62	136	145	8	11
Cautín	38	46	118	7	6
Valdivia	66	115	146	16	14
Osorno	102	146	165	8	9
Llanquihue	110	140	190	16	20
Chiloé	28	36	48	4	6
Aysen	30	46	48	2	4
Magallanes	58	96	115	9	11
Totals	2,376	4,015	5,621	337	398 = 12,747

Source: Sección: Registro y Evaluación, Depto. de Organizaciones, Consejería Nacional de Promoción Popular.

J.V.   Juntas de Vecinos (neighborhood groups)
C.M.   Centros de Madres (mothers' centers)
C.D.   Centros Deportivos (sports centers)
O.J.   Organizaciones Juveniles (youth organizations)
C.C.A.   Clubes Culturales y Artísticos (art and culture clubs)
* Included are those enjoying legal personality, as of June, 1966.

parties to their left received 37 per cent of the vote. In 1965 the shift of votes was dramatic. These same groups of parties received 26 per cent and 67 per cent of the votes respectively.

TABLE 5

GROWTH OF POPULAR DEVELOPMENT ORGANIZATIONS
IN SECTIONS OF FOUR PROVINCES*

Year Group	Number of New Organizations Created
1925–29	18
1930–34	17
1935–39	31
1940–44	68
1945–49	90
1950–54	141
1955–59	239
1960–64	987
1965–66	734
	2,325

Source: Sección: Registro y Evaluación, Depto. de Organizaciones, Consejería Nacional de Promoción Popular.

* Based on information available from tax records of organizations for parts of the provinces of Antofagasta, Santiago, Valdivia and Osorno.

Certain Operational Considerations and Proposals

A few factors which heavily influence development should be mentioned as background to specific action proposals.

First, foreign aid, particularly U.S. aid, has emphasized physical plant while tending to stress, insufficiently, the human element. Strained relations between U.S. and Chilean officials have been caused by U.S. insistence upon public identification of the source of funds.

Second, the infusion of aid seems not adequately to consider the capability of the Chilean government to absorb and administer it. Aid should be accompanied by technical assistance for the training of personnel in the recipient organization and to assist in the monitoring of the use of funds.

Third, a great amount of political and social development, particularly among the non-integrated part of the population has been diverted to heading off agitation and violence, and to preventing extreme political action. It now is necessary to channel energies into positive constructive programs.

Fourth is the consideration that traditional organizations tend to be inward looking and untrusting; evasiveness rather than frankness and honesty is a common tactic.

With these circumstances in mind, we suggest a few efforts which would, if implemented, contribute to the long-range strategy for the development of improved public administration of Chile.

1) Much more detailed knowledge of family life is necessary in order to plan the types of activities necessary to start successful, effective preschool programs.[4] In addition to knowledge of the family situation, an analysis should be made of the qualitative and quantitative output of present social worker and nursery-school teacher training programs.

2) A serious classroom space gap exists. Supplementary financing and technical assistance for school construction would significantly increase educational opportunities.

3) In primary and secondary education, the social sciences and civics require extensive curriculum development. Financial and technical assistance is needed to research, write, and publish Chilean social science texts and workbooks.

A recent effective pilot project in learning materials development trained a group to work on the project. This team studied abroad and sharpened its abilities, as a team, to write primary school readers.

4) At the level of university education, in those institutions where an interest in empirical research is found, every reasonable measure should be taken to strengthen it and relate it to course work. Students should be encouraged to participate in research projects; a system of research and teaching assistantships could serve as the vehicle. Assistance in the acquisition and interfaculty utilization of equipment for research would also be of considerable value.

5) The need to expose Latin American students to the realities of government is very great. This can be done through internships for outstanding students, perhaps to work on government projects on a part-time basis. To a very limited extent the School of

[4] One prototype program is that of the Sweet Memorial Day Care Center, operated in slum sections of Santiago. Its children come from homes where the average monthly income is less than $30, yet 80 per cent of its "alumni" finish their primary education, far exceeding the national average.

Political and Administrative Sciences has already tried this approach.

6) The quality of administrative preparation both for functional specialists and for lower level personnel needs more attention. INSORA's rich and varied consulting experiences should enable it to develop a program of studies for students of other professional schools which could be given by INSORA personnel or by the teaching staff of the professional school.

Although the regional programs are aimed toward lower-middle level administrators, the Faculty of Economic Sciences in Santiago seeks to produce ministers and heads of autonomous services and the School of Political and Administrative Sciences, sub-ministers and assistant directors of services. Neither of the latter two is interested in middle and lower management personnel. The high school graduate or former college student who drifts into the lower branches of this *técnico* level, if given two years of specialized training, could be much better prepared for his job. It may require the incentive of foreign support to generate action in this area since it is one with little popular appeal.

7) The programs in the public sector for the non-integrated individual are aimed primarily toward meeting housing and educational needs. On the whole the education programs are well conceived and executed. But when the educationally rehabilitated individual terminates his classes, he may be caught in a reading ability gap. His skills may not be adequate to digest available publications. A program is needed to provide interesting, useful, timely reading materials designed to fit the special reading skills of this category of citizens.

8) It is obvious, as demands for medical services mount, that drastic changes are necessary in the education of doctors, nurses, and public health officials. This would require an overhaul of the system of preparing medical and public health personnel, the revised program to stress relevant technical content, the development of professional attitudes, and an understanding of the social functions of medicine and medical services.

With respect to improving some elements of health administration, it is encouraging that the Pan American Health Organization has established a continuing sixteen-week course in administration for top and middle level Latin American health ministry personnel. The program is being conducted by INSORA in collaboration with the Chilean Ministry of Public Health.

THE NATURE OF POLITICAL COMPETITION

The citizenry of Chile work through various types of organizations to communicate their interests to those with political power. The political parties, the chambers of commerce, the various farmers' organizations, the bar associations, and the national industrialists' society are among the organizations which make up the structure of political competition.

Political Parties

Prior to the 1860's, the political system was so dominated by presidential authority that the role of political parties was extremely limited. Following separation from Spain in 1817, Chile found herself free of all political ties, but with her Spanish-oriented social structure intact.[5]

During the period between 1830 and 1871 the government was "a traditional authority, a quiet and silent force, loyally obeyed and respected, eternal, above any caudillos and factions."[6] Government was the executive which had no effective "counterweight." The political issues of the day were "synthesized principally in the conflict between two organic spiritual elements, both of which belonged to the past: the aristocracy and the monarchy."[7]

After mid-century Chile experienced remarkable economic growth, primarily because of mining activities. As wealth spread, movements for civil liberties, freedom of suffrage, secularization, and limitation of executive authority began to appear.[8] About this time political parties emerged, crystallizing around liberal ideas and rightist, status quo elements. By 1891 the split in the aristoc-

[5] Federico G. Gil, *Genesis and Modernization of Political Parties in Chile* (Gainesville: University of Florida Press, 1962), 5.

[6] *Ibid.*, 6.

[7] Alberto Edwards, *La Fronda Aristocratica* (Santiago de Chile: Editorial del Pacifico: 1962), 15.

[8] Gil, *Political Parties*, 10.

racy culminated in a brief civil war over the issue of whether a strong executive, representing the aristocracy, was to control or whether parliamentary power was to mediate.

After the civil war seven parties were in existence and coalition government was the rule. The instability and administrative chaos (121 different cabinets in the thirty-three years between 1891 and 1925) led in 1925 to a military takeover. A new constitution was written containing several significant political changes. First, congressional members were elected through a system of proportional representation. Secondly, the president was to be selected by congress should any candidate fail to receive a majority of the popular votes. But as Gil points out, proportional representation has encouraged party fragmentation and unstable congressional coalitions.[9]

By 1949, ten parties were represented in Congress, and an additional ten new parties had been registered for congressional elections. In the 1953 congressional elections, no less than thirty-eight political organizations had candidates running for office. In the 1954 congressional election, the number was reduced to eighteen, and in the 1958 presidential elections four candidates ran for office.

It is not surprising that in this volatile environment no sustained concern for effective administration was to be found. In 1933 significant administrative changes were made in connection with reform of the constitution. Agencies were created outside the control of the president and the ministries. Soon after, further decentralization occurred through the creation of semi-autonomous fiscal institutions and state industries. These organizations operated under the control of *consejos* or boards of directors which were solely responsible.

Current observers refer to this period as the time when the roots of Chile's "administrative anarchy" were laid down.

In general, interest groups in Chile, such as the Chamber of Commerce, National Agrarian Society, and the Federation of Educational Institutions do not have specific proposals for improving the conduct of the public service. Criticisms of the public service abound, but there is an absence of positive programs and

9 *Ibid.,* 28.

policies around which the efforts of these groups might coalesce. Brief discussions with some of the leadership of these groups suggest the nature of attitudes toward the public service.

Chambers of Commerce

The president of the Chamber of Commerce praises the efficiency of the Central Bank and of the public service in general. He centers his criticism on the customs office, suggesting that the quality of personnel could be improved if the pay were better. Nevertheless, he reports that members of the Exporters' Association of Chile and the Customs Office, assisted by an AID-financed technical assistance team have, over the past two years, simplified procedures and improved efficiency by an estimated 80 per cent.

The demands of the work situation and pressures for change from within and without, he feels, will be sufficient to obtain improved performance. He criticizes the government's tax policy but praises the tax bureau's effectiveness in collecting taxes. He feels that the ability of the Chamber to present its point of view on tax issues is severely limited by its lack of research personnel.

National Agrarian Society

The National Agrarian Society is an association of farmers of large and medium-sized land holdings, which, collectively, account for 80 per cent of agricultural production. It supports agricultural experimentation and research, provides extension services to its members, and is presently engaged in the first stage of a major study of all aspects of farm management and productivity.

The president of the society has questioned the ability of the Ministry of Agriculture to plan, given the "erroneous and incomplete statistical data available." He feels the Ministry is not well staffed because of low compensation rates. He believes that agriculture must revert to the private sector if there is to be increased food production. Legitimate governmental activities in the agricultural sector should be limited to the control of diseases and to inspection of production, which he says "the government people do quite well." Interest in reform is expressed more as a desire to redefine the functions of government than to improve its efficiency.

Federation of Educational Institutions

The Federation represents private educational institutions and receives most of its support from Catholic schools. It has a department of educational services and research, a department concerned with obtaining and maintaining government support to private schools, an editorial department, and a division for research on training techniques. The Federation's president says that the Ministry of Education plans without consulting or informing the private educational sector. Great interest was expressed in maintaining policies supportive of private education.

National Association of Public Administrators

The Association membership consists of the 350 graduates of the University of Chile's School of Political Science which was begun in 1958. Sixty per cent of the graduates are now in the executive branch of the government; 25 per cent are in the private sector; most of the remainder are professors, lawyers, or military officers.

The Association, which draws its authority from a presidential decree, is concerned with improving education for the public service through participation in special commissions set up by the rector of the University of Chile. The Association backs no general administrative reforms, but its president emphasizes the need to eliminate from many laws the detailed organizational and administrative provisions which now encumber them.

Certain Operational Considerations and Proposals

On the surface it would seem unadvisable to suggest that any assistance to political parties or pressure groups might be undertaken. However, two factors merit reflection on this possibility. First, the wide panorama of programs undertaken by the government, with considerable foreign assistance, has committed all political parties, regardless of their ideologies, to continued support of popularly oriented programs. The expectations of the populace have been awakened and will need to be served, putting great demands upon the resources of the parties. Secondly, party youth, increasingly university educated, are achieving higher levels of technical training and political sophistication, making them potentially better users of foreign assistance.

Specific proposals for strengthening public administration are:

Support of conferences on public issues, with representation from the public and private sectors, to improve communications and to identify issues calling for the cooperation of these groups;

Support of seminars and workshops on administrative improvement in specific functional fields such as health or social security to which party leaders, foreign and national professionals, and individuals from the private sector are invited; and

Within the Congress where the major parties have commissions paralleling regular standing committees, the establishment of research or staff assistantships, for the party commissions, to be granted to promising university students.

ASPECTS OF GOVERNMENTAL STRUCTURE

The Congress

Each of the houses of Congress has an administrative service for editing and legislative reference, and each provides staff services for its committees. In addition, a common library serves both houses.

The changing nature of the legislature, from conservative to leftist with an action orientation, has put an increased burden upon the information and staff services. Furthermore, since the executive branch has become the originator of an ever-increasing number of bills, the legislature is under pressure to analyze executive proposals. The traditional suspicion of the executive also causes an additional research burden, particularly in the Senate, where the Administration party does not have a majority and where the analyses of proposals are more rigorous.

Each of the standing committees of Congress has a secretary, usually a lawyer, responsible for providing professional staff services. Most secretaries serve more than one committee. Lack of sufficient professional and reference personnel results in the individual legislator's having to obtain his own information in government offices, which must, by law, provide it upon request. However, when legislators personally come seeking and demanding information, the consequence tends to be an accumulation of unfulfilled requests and a deterioration in relationships between the branches of government. Part of the congestion stems from a need to modernize procedures, and particularly to codify the legislation previously adopted.

Congress as yet has been unable to find the time to reorganize and improve its internal services. Four specific improvements in the internal operations of the legislature are suggested:

1) The codification and indexing of all laws. This could be done by the law schools.

2) The congressional library should be organized more effectively to serve legislators and great amounts of unused material could be reallocated to other libraries.

3) A study of internal congressional organization and procedures should be undertaken.

4) Adequate staff services and appropriate physical facilities should be provided for each committee.

The Executive

Under the Chilean constitution the president can create law by executive decree subject to review by the Congress and by the Contraloria General.[10] This power was made operative in 1942 with the passage of Law No. 7200, which came from a presidential request for greater "legislative" autonomy in administrative and economic matters. Prior to this, while the president was chief administrator of the country, he was severely limited by congressional inaction.

[10] The Contraloria General is autonomous. "Its purpose is to supervise the income and investment of fiscal funds, of the Municipalidades and of

A second type of "legislative" action available to the executive is found in administrative regulations. They are complements to the law and, like the decree, have the force of law. A third source is executive instruction through which the executive implements, corrects, or complements laws and decrees. As in the case of decrees, regulations and instruction must be reviewed for legality and constitutionality by the Contraloria General.

The Executive has, in the opinion of some observers, undertaken administrative reform with laws so complicated and legalistic that the snarl of red tape, or *tramitación,* has clogged the government's machinery. The overwhelming majority of laws bearing on the public administration of Chile have been enacted by executive action including the establishment of each of the ministries. The cry is now being raised that constitutional reform is necessary to correct what is called this "administrative anarchy."

The question can be asked: Why has not the decree power available to the executive been used to clear away the obstacles. To answer the question the organizational structure within the executive branch needs to be understood. It is divided into two main sectors, the centralized and the decentralized. In the centralized sector are the fourteen ministries and the Office of the President. The decentralized sector makes a distinction between the sectors functionally and territorially decentralized. In the latter group are the municipalities and the provincial administrators.[11] In the functionally decentralized sector are the fiscal and semifiscal institutions, service and state industries.

The *fiscales,* which are usually commercial in character, have their own sources of income and are not financed through annual budget appropriations, although their capital is derived from public

---

Public Beneficiency; verify the examination and consolidation of accounts to be rendered by persons who are in charge of funds and goods of the previously mentioned entities and of the services and institutions submitted by law to supervision and inspection of the corresponding offices; keep the general accounting of the country; express its opinion over the constitutionality and legality of the supreme decrees; supervise the fulfillment of the dispositions of Administrative status and perform all the functions assigned by law."
Manual de la Organización del Gobierno de Chile, Dirección de Presupuestos (1960), 535.

[11] Although the constitution provides for the election of Provincial Assemblies to serve as legislative complements to the presidentially appointed provincial governors, this has never been put into effect.

sources. They have a special legal personality, and while not entirely independent of government control, have considerable autonomy. Their personnel are not public employees in a strict sense; hence, for example, they can receive pay raises without special legislation.

The *semi-fiscal* institutions are the same as the *fiscales* except that they enjoy less autonomy. These agencies are listed under the various ministries, but in some cases the number of their employees far exceeds the employees in the ministerial offices. Witness the Ministry of Public Health, which has fifteen "centralized" employees versus 44,053 "decentralized" employees. Table 6 presents a classification of public service personnel by relationship to ministries.

Once created and beyond budgetary influence, the autonomous agencies become powerful islands of self-perpetuating interest. Over a period of thirty years there has been a growth of organizations whose functions overlap and are duplicating. At present there are twenty-one separate organizations working on agrarian reform. No fewer than fifty social security institutions serve the public.

The various agencies operate autonomous personnel systems with differing pay scales, employee rights and benefits, and operating procedures. The result is rigidity in the movement of personnel from agency to agency so that the personnel resources of one organization cannot even temporarily be considered as potential resources for other agencies.

Solution to the problem of structural anarchy, as it might be called, will come gradually: through the establishment of a civil service commission; through centralization of budgeting controls; through pressures created by rapidly changing technology; through the awakening of a sense of political and economic responsibility by advisory boards in the autonomous agencies; and through the growing professionalization of staff.

A second aspect of the Executive is the system of bureaucratic action, bound up in organic laws and regulations written in detailed legal fashion rigidly establishing operating procedures, which in some instances can only be changed by law. Traditionalism encourages a tight formalistic control symbolized by the rubber stamp and signature. While the Contraloria General is charged with

TABLE 6
CLASSIFICATION OF PUBLIC SERVICE PERSONNEL BY RELATIONSHIP
TO THE MINISTRIES

A. Personnel dependent on ministries:

Ministries	Central-ized Insti-tutions	Decen-tralized Insti-tutions	Total Ministries Personnel	Percentages Central-ized Insti-tutions	Decen-tralized Insti-tutions
Interior	33,263	—	33,263	100.0	—
Foreign Affairs	307	—	307	100.0	—
Econ. Dev. and Rec.	1,142	35,895	37,037	3.1	96.9
Finance	7,015	5,186	12,301	57.0	43.0
Public Education	51,894	9,790	61,684	84.1	15.9
Justice	4,757	—	4,757	100.0	—
War	37,826	—	37,826	100.0	—
Public Works	11,239	2,307	13,546	82.9	17.1
Agriculture	2,973	—	2,973	100.0	—
Lands and Coloniz.	528	—	528	100.0	—
Work and Soc. Sec.	446	6,488	6,934	6.4	93.6
Public Health	15	44,053	44,068	0.0	100.0
Mining	107	1,533	1,640	0.1	99.9
Total	151,512	105,252	256,864	58.9	41.1

B. Personnel not dependent on ministries:

Institution	Number of Persons
Presidency of the Republic	87
Contraloria General	705
Municipalities	15,379
Congress	528
Judicial Power	1,667
Total	18,366

Source: Adapted from: Instituto de Administración, *Recursos Humanos de la Administración Pública Chilena,* Santiago de Chile, 1962.

the responsibility of verifying the legality of regulations and decrees, it is frequently not attuned to the functional purposes being sought. This, coupled with the fact that the Contraloria participates in the review process at a very late stage in the preparation of proposals, results in attention to legal form rather than substance.

Thus legalistic formalism becomes perpetuated and delegation of authority and responsibility to lower bureaucratic levels is blocked. Bureaucratic action becomes procedure oriented rather than activity or goal oriented. Bureaucratic decision making is concentrated in a few offices and produces a congestion of activities and a constant pressure for expediting delayed projects. One serious consequence of this pressure is the lack of attention given to planning and evaluation of activities and resource usage.

In May, 1965, the President designated what may become the most important body for improvement of public administration, the Comisión Especial de Racionalización de la Administración Civil del Estado. It is headed by the Controller General and has among its members the Ministerial Secretary and Subsecretary from the Office of the Presidency and the Subsecretaries of Interior, Finance, Education, and Justice. Its objective is to study and recommend to the President measures for the improvement, simplification, and greater efficiency of government services. It has been the responsible agent for several significant pieces of legislation.

Under Law No. 16,436 of 1966, the procedural stumbling block caused by the requirement for ministerial signatures on most documents began to crumble. The law gave ministers and top government officials the authority to delegate this task. The partial success achieved by this law has encouraged the Commission to seek means of even more widely diffusing responsibility.

Another important project is the adoption of the *jornada continua de trabajo,* which limits the midday break and makes for greater continuity in the work day.

The Commission has also been responsible for the creation of information, claims, and suggestion offices in government agencies; for the establishment of periodic meetings among top government officials to discuss administrative problems; for achieving greater control over much-abused sick leave practices; for measures to control the use, cost, and maintenance of government vehicles; and other lesser actions.

Under study are proposals to strengthen organizations and management offices in the ministries; reorganize the social security system; expedite the procedures for installing new industries; rationalize and standardize administrative procedures; and undertake in-service training programs for government officials.

The tasks to be undertaken by this Commission exceed its staff resources. Given the outstanding quality of this group and the importance of its work with respect to the improvement of public administration, increased assistance should be made available to it.

The third aspect of the Executive is its size and the quality of its personnel system. The government of Chile has the highest percentage of public employees in Latin America, 13.9 per cent of the employed population. Basic personnel problems seem to revolve around inadequate pay and training. In the professional fields it is difficult for the government to compete with the substantially higher salaries being offered by the private sector. One consequence of low salaries is that many government officials hold two or more "full-time" positions.

The lack of a civil service system has resulted not only in uneven pay rates but also in a promotion system which is not usually based on merit. Although the Administrative Statute calls for five promotions based on merit to one based on seniority, actual practice is nearly the reverse.

There are prospects that new civil service legislation may be forthcoming. The Central Office of Organization and Methods (OCOM) located in the Ministry of Finance has recently completed, with the assistance of a United Nations expert, a six-year task of classifying over 175,000 jobs in more than 800 separate job descriptions. Out of this effort has come a unified pay scale which presently covers most of the public employees in the centralized agencies. Legislation has been drafted which would create a civil service commission and extend the equal pay for equal work concept to the entire public sector. Machinery to regulate a government-wide merit promotion system is called for as well as a national in-service training program. However, the political climate has been unfavorable for the presentation of the legislation.

Action Proposals with Respect to Training

In turning to suggestions particularly related to training, several considerations substantially affect the strategies to be followed. In the period between 1962 and 1965 the United States spent more than $560 million for Chilean development. Less than $2 million was devoted to strengthening the administrative capability of the Chilean government. One residual of foreign aid should be trained, professional personnel, improved procedures, and effective, timely programs capable ultimately of being staffed by local personnel. While this goal is sought by AID in its technical assistance efforts, it appears that too little attention is in fact given to how the goal can be met.

The government's own program of economic and social reform severely taxes the administrative capabilities of the executive, legislative, and judicial branches of government. In consideration of this the present administration is preparing a bill to create a civil service authority for the purpose of standardizing salaries, making promotions a function of merit, and creating a national public administration training institute. The government, recognizing how significant the training need is, would provide facilities for classes and staff and would offer sufficient incentives to assure that the best qualified may be encouraged to attend training classes. Existing training programs, with few exceptions, fail to impart a sense of urgency with respect to social and administrative change.

A proposal made to representatives of USAID, the Ford Foundation, and the government of Chile to establish an interim training program until the above legislation is adopted would make use of the considerable interest and talent existing within the universities of Chile. Faculty members would be called upon to serve as advisers and instructors for training courses, supplemented by assistance from government personnel.

The suggested training program would include a series of high-level conferences on executive leadership for ministers, subsecretaries, and congressmen. The objectives would be to first enlarge the knowledge of senior officials with regard to the nation's social and economic development and to generate attitudes leading to more effective administrative action and leadership. Second, a by-product might be more sympathetic understanding of the need for training in government generally.

Courses would be offered in Santiago for personnel at the higher levels of administration and management (i.e., the top seven grades of Chilean bureaucracy). Possible specialized courses might include program budgeting, preparation and implementation of development projects, personnel administration, regional planning, legislative processes, promotion of private sector investment, administrative law, and methods of organizing and managing agencies and units.

Specialized courses would be given in the provinces, perhaps in combination with University of Chile regional colleges and provincial universities to cover such subjects as regional planning, urban problems, municipal government, and community development.

The training program would not actually offer training for personnel at lower levels, but would assist the ministries in developing and implementing courses in such subjects as public accounting and statistics, customs administration, purchasing and supply, documentation and filing, secretarial skills, public health administration, and other subjects required by lower level personnel in ministries, Congress, or the judiciary.

An effort would be made at all levels to develop a sense of professionalism and public purpose. Such a program must be grounded in the reality of public administration in Chile. In order that the "feel" of reality may be gained through firsthand experience, it is essential that instructors be engaged in applied empirical research and data gathering. Thus it is essential to have research as an aspect of the training.

CONCLUSION

The strategies presented here for the improvement of public administration are based upon the view that unless attitudes are changed through the processes of political socialization and competition, responses will continue to be in terms of conditions and values which existed a generation ago. If the citizenry is not capable of articulating needs and evaluating programs, the democratic process will wither and the bureaucratic process will become stagnant.

In the developing situation found in most Latin American

countries, the inability of governments to meet urgent social and economic needs has resulted in foreign technical and financial assistance.

The size of the assistance must not be determined by the aspirations of either the recipient or the donor, nor by the capacity of the recipient to absorb the assistance. Rather, it should be based upon careful analysis of the activity needs to achieve mutually agreed upon goals. If the capacity of the recipient is not sufficient to absorb the assistance, then a sub-assistance for creating that capacity must be considered an integral part of the assistance program.

The size of the assistance effort must be determined by the capacity of the recipient to absorb.

The donating agencies should operate through the foreign assistance "clearing house" activities of the National Planning Office. Only in this way will it be possible to make planned attacks upon priority problems.

The donating agency needs to develop a system for accumulating, storing, retrieving, analyzing, and disseminating the experience and knowledge gained by its staff. This applies equally to USAID, the Ford Foundation, university exchange programs, etc.

Cognizance needs to be taken of the different perspectives on problem-solving found in the United States, and in many parts of Latin America. The approach in the former tends to be pragmatic and limited; in the latter, "world restructuring" and idealistic.

Donor organizations must be willing to accept long-range commitments if permanent effects are to result. The present policy of limited-term contracts to completely change major organizations is unrealistic.

Technical assistance personnel should commit themselves to stay with projects until completion, or to the completion of important stages.

Whenever feasible, Chilean organizations receiving assistance should organize special teams of personnel to work with the assistance program, should send the team abroad for specialized study in appropriate fields, and should maintain the team as a functioning unit after the completion of the assistance in order to retrain or supervise other groups.

Peru

JAMES R. HIMES

INTRODUCTION

Honey's essay, by adopting a broad definition of public administration and stressing the importance of long-run educational programs for the preparation of public administrators, requires that country studies, which follow the outline delineated, also take a broad view. Attention is drawn especially to the role which should be played by the universities, secondary schools, and presumably also primary schools, families, churches, and other agencies of "political socialization" in forming citizens' attitudes toward and knowledge of their governments and the public service. It would be overly ambitious for this commentary to try to put such a broad range of institutions in Peru into the perspective of Dr. Honey's framework. Primary attention here will be given to the importance of post-secondary education and training since it is at this level that foreign assistance is most likely to be directed. One of the conclusions which can be drawn, however, is that a great deal more attention needs to be paid to primary and secondary education by way of developing positive attitudes toward the "process of conduct of the public service" if the quality of public administration is to be improved significantly in Latin America.

It might be noted in passing that it is unlikely that important results at the primary and secondary levels will be obtained merely by attempts to improve courses in civic education or the introduction of more social studies material. Much more important is the initiation or extension of teaching methods which stimulate inquisitiveness, accustom the students to learning from reading and observation, and generate organizational and analytical skills.

At the post-secondary level, the most relevant institutions for training related to public administration are the universities, public

141

administration training institutes, and the various ministries and public agencies themselves. Each of these institutions should have a distinct focus in the education for public affairs which it provides. Dr. Honey suggests that the general inadequacy of social science education in the universities is perhaps the most inhibiting educational barrier blocking the effective development of public administration in Latin America.

Social Science Education in the Peruvian Universities

There can be little doubt that the state of social science education in Peru restricts the availability of highly qualified administrators for the public service. Equally or more important, however, and a point which will receive more attention later, is the general lack of orientation toward public problems in university education in Peru. An uncomfortable air of mutual suspicion often prevails between the governmental bureaucracy and the Peruvian universities. The universities generally fear that entangling alliances with public ministries will jeopardize their autonomy, while governmental agencies frequently resist collaboration with the universities to avoid becoming embroiled in "politics." This problem is not only restricted to the social sciences but also arises in other disciplines related to public administration, such as engineering, medicine, and agriculture.

The social sciences in Latin American universities have not fared well under the professionalized faculty system which characterizes most of these institutions. It is at once the area of study where interdisciplinary instruction and research is of the utmost importance, while at the same time the various disciplines commonly regarded as making up the social sciences are widely scattered among faculties of economics, law, letters, and various "schools" and "institutes" which are either independent or part of the above faculties.

There are in Peru a growing number of "faculties of social sciences." Among the more important universities, the agrarian university at La Molina, Catholic University, and the University "San Cristobal de Huamanga" at Ayacucho each has its Facultad de

Ciencias Sociales. Only at La Molina, however, is all of the social science material which is offered in the University taught at this one faculty. But La Molina is primarily an agrarian university and might be expected to have an important impact only on that sector of the public service related to agriculture. The other universities with social science faculties have typically separate faculties of "economic sciences," which normally offer study programs in accounting, economics, and administration. The university at Huancayo goes so far as to have, in addition to a Faculty of Social Sciences, a Faculty of Economics and a Faculty of "Public and Private Administration."

In the Peruvian setting, it would not appear advisable to encourage the establishment of more social science faculties in an effort to provide the kind of educational background required for many professionals in public affairs. In most cases, such faculties are unlikely to be able to absorb the economics curriculum since the economics faculties are generally among the largest and most independent in the Peruvian universities. It may also prove difficult to wrest from the law faculties the responsibility which they often have, however unrealized, for limited aspects of political science instruction.

More realistic than structural reform of the Peruvian university by creation, elimination, or rearrangement of faculties is the introduction of more inter-faculty flexibility into the curriculum, i.e., permitting, or requiring, the interested student to take relevant courses offered by different faculties in order to develop a social science "program." This kind of curriculum reform is of course related to, but not necessarily dependent upon, the introduction of "general studies" or liberal arts programs into the first two of Peru's five years of university study. General studies programs of one sort or another are currently in the planning stages at the universities of San Marcos, Trujillo, Arequipa, and Catholic University, but the implementation of these programs will require much time and effort and considerable financial backing. The success of the credit system and "core courses," which have already been established at La Molina, hopefully will provide additional incentives to other universities to accelerate their own programs.

A special problem arises in Peru in the quest for appropriate ways to introduce modern political science material into the university curriculum. With respect to the administrative sciences, law, sociology, and social anthropology, while the teaching of these subjects may be unrelated to the developmental problems of Peru, there is at least an institutional framework into which development-oriented material may be introduced. Such is not the case with political science, a discipline which virtually does not exist in this country. It is true that a number of law faculties carry the addendum "y ciencias politicas" on their official titles, but there is no substance to this term other than a few courses descriptive of legal and political institutions which are normally included in any law curriculum. There are no Peruvian political scientists who employ a behavioral or "civic culture" approach to the subject.

Given the state of affairs of political science in Peru, it is doubtful that it makes sense for foreign assistance agencies (and the initiative surely will not come from within) to seek to develop academic political science institutions as such. It is questionable that a viable political science department could be established in the near future in a Peruvian university. One such effort has recently been undertaken by the Catholic University in Lima, and it will be interesting to follow the progress of this venture. In most Peruvian universities, however, particularly the public ones, it will almost certainly be necessary to work with the established faculties and departments in developing some elements of political science education. With the addition of several capable and appropriately trained professors, a good background in political science could be provided by building on programs already operative in faculties and departments of law, sociology, and economics. There should be no insurmountable difficulty in this endeavor if the kind of curriculum flexibility mentioned above is introduced. The faculties of law might be expected to provide the political science courses having a descriptive and institutional approach, and the faculties of economics to provide those courses dealing with public administration, and sociology or anthropology departments the more behaviorally and culturally oriented material. It appears that those most likely to be interested in the civic culture approach to political science in Peru are the few sociologists or social anthropologists, particularly at La Molina, the Institute of Peruvian Studies, and Catholic University, who have had some exposure to current developments in U.S. political sociology and political science.

The establishment of non-degree-offering institutes of political studies in a few of the Peruvian universities which already have some competence in related fields might create the appropriate environment for professional contact among the various professors of administration, law, economics, sociology, and anthropology who have interests in some aspects of political science. Such institutes could, when established, serve also as a source of pressure for the inclusion of optional core courses in political science (although they might not be so called) and an eventual specialization in political science in the plans for curriculum reform and general studies programs which are currently being considered by a number of important Peruvian universities.

Although political science in Peru is undoubtedly the least developed of the social sciences, the impression should not be left that the other disciplines in this field are now at a stage where they are making significant contributions to public administration development (or general economic and social development) in this country. In fact, with the exception of the field of agricultural economics at La Molina and anthropology at the Institute of Peruvian Studies (which is independent of any university), it is difficult to point out a program in the social sciences in Peru which really presents at this time a solid opportunity for foreign assistance. An experimental program for improving economics teaching and research in Peru is described later.

ONRAP

Outside the universities, public administration training and research institutions provide another important opportunity for the development of human resources for the civil service. In Peru, the Oficina Nacional de Racionalización y Capacitación de la Administración Pública (ONRAP) was established by Supreme Decree in April, 1964, from two already existing organizations: the Peruvian Public Administration Institute, created in 1958, and the Office of Administrative Organization and Rationalization of the National Planning Institute. ONRAP is charged with four general responsibilities: (1) the study and recommendation of the objectives and means of public administration reform, (2) the training of civil servants in the techniques of public administration, (3) the coordination of studies related to the structure and functioning of the public institutions and the approval of any structural reform of these institutions, and (4) the establishment of organization and methods offices in governmental agencies.

ONRAP is governed by a Consejo Directivo which consists of the Ministers of Finance and Justice or their delegates, the head of the National Planning Institute or his delegate, and two representatives from the private sector. The chief executive officer is the president of the Consejo, until recently Victor Miranda Nieto, who was appointed by the President of the Republic shortly after the establishment of ONRAP.

The Office has three program divisions which reflect the primary activities of ONRAP: the *Dirección de Investigaciónes Normativas,* which undertakes research for the most part in connection with technical assistance projects and the preparation of teaching materials; the *Dirección de Programas Aplicados,* which is in charge of providing technical assistance to Peruvian governmental agencies (organization and methods, personnel policy, economic analysis, and accounting); and the *Dirección de Capacitación* or Training Division.

The Training Division of ONRAP so far has organized courses primarily for middle-level civil servants, although some programs have been initiated for senior executives in public organizations and also for lower level personnel. The courses offered during the 1966 academic year (April to December) are the following: Administración Pública para Jefes; Administración de Personal; Organización y Métodos; Presupuesto Funcional; Abastecimientos y Archivo; Secretariado Administrativo; and Administración de la Documentación. These courses are generally of one semester, with four to nine hours a week of class work. The course "Administración para Jefes" consists, however, of twenty class hours per week.

There are now about eighty-five staff members at ONRAP, approximately one-third of whom are professional personnel (not including a number of teachers hired on a part-time basis). Five to seven professionals have been maintained on the AID-financed Institute of Public Administration (IPA) Mission at ONRAP. AID had originally contracted IPA in January, 1963, to provide technical assistance to the Peruvian Public Administration Institute, but the collaboration continued and became more substantial with the establishment of ONRAP. AID's financial assistance currently amounts to about $400,000 per year. The total AID/IPA project with ONRAP will probably amount to about $1,600,000 and is scheduled to run until 1968.

Created by a decree of the President of Peru and not by act of Congress, ONRAP's legal and economic position is somewhat tenuous at the present time. This year the Peruvian government's direct contribution to ONRAP's operating budget amounted to slightly less than $90,000. The institution has been forced to depend to a large extent upon contracts with public agencies for financing research and extension projects, putting the selection of these projects on the basis of ability to pay rather than relevance to the country's development needs. These problems have also made more difficult the important task of developing an experienced and permanent professional staff at ONRAP.

The most immediate concern of ONRAP's leadership indeed appears to be the shortage of capable professional personnel to work on the increasing number of requests for technical assistance on structural and organizational matters which ONRAP receives from public organizations. The difficulty of securing such personnel results both from budgetary limitations and from the scarcity of qualified people in Peru to undertake such assignments. This scarcity is, of course, intimately related to the weakness of university training, particularly in the social sciences, to which Dr. Honey draws attention.

Given the weakness or absence of pre-service and in-service training for public administration in Peru, ONRAP runs the risk, in developing its own training program, of attempting to adopt stop-gap measures to fill the voids left by inadequate university instruction in fields related to public administration and unsatisfactory training programs in the various ministries. With its capacity for about three hundred students and with continuing budgetary problems, ONRAP cannot and should not attempt to take on the responsibility of pre-service training for public organizations nor of specific job-related training that should be provided by the ministries. ONRAP rather should direct its training efforts to the preparation of "teachers of trainers" for the training programs of the various ministries and to executive development programs for senior civil servants.

A course entitled "Administración para Graduados" was supposed to have been offered to full-time students by ONRAP in 1966 in part to make up for the absence of adequate pre-service training in the Peruvian universities. As it turned out, there was not sufficient interest in the course on the part of capable students to merit its being taught. This experience illustrates the difficulty of attempting to provide a sort of remedial course in public administration to "reach" students who are already graduates of universities and have recently begun their careers. This sort of basic material must be taught in a university setting, and in the long run ONRAP would be well advised to assist in the efforts to upgrade public administration instruction in the universities rather than trying to create substitutes for such training.

The Ministries

In addition to the Peruvian universities and ONRAP, the various governmental agencies also present opportunities for the development of training programs in public administration. It is extraordinary, however, how little attention has been given to organizing such programs. Only the Ministries of Public Health and Foreign Affairs and the armed forces have training divisions charged with orientation and in-service training. It is doubtful that ONRAP, for its part, can adequately perform its training functions until training divisions are established in all the most important ministries and until it is assured that qualified persons, in sufficient numbers, are released by the government to undertake the kind of training, both in Peru and abroad, which they will need in order to be able to carry out successful orientation and in-service training programs in the ministries.

Government and the Universities in Peru

James R. Watson, former chief of party of the AID/Institute of Public Administration Mission in Peru, wrote in his end-of-tour report:

Given the necessity for governmental interest and support,

the long tradition of university abstinence from governmental affairs, the intense involvement of some university students and professors in partisan political activities and protest movements, and the lack of university interest in developing curricula to prepare students for public service, the prospect of developing an effective public administration improvement organization with a university base, in my opinion, continues to be remote, and, in the Peruvian context, undesirable.

There can be no doubt that in Peru there has been a "long tradition of university abstinence from government affairs," but this deplorable tradition is also related to an equally unfortunate lack of *constructive* governmental interest in university affairs. No Peruvian government, in recent years at least, has sought consciously and determinedly to develop the competence of universities in fields related to the government's own development plans. It is not the purpose here to place the blame on either the government or the universities but rather on both. The universities must begin to take pride in serving national objectives by collaborating with government agencies and not view every such collaboration as a threat to their sacred "autonomy." The Peruvian public institutions, for their part, would do well not to be fooled into thinking that because there are periodic disturbances and even turmoil in the universities, that there is no serious scholarship under way within these institutions. Scholarship does not make the headlines the way that strikes, student elections, and demonstrations do. It is also a mistake to assume that all the public universities in Peru are "embroiled in politics." Actually there is a rather striking disinterest in national and international politics on the part of many, probably a majority, of Peruvian students and professors. It is also important to differentiate between activist interest on the part of the students and professors in crucial issues facing the university, which in Peru is understandably strong, and political problems facing the nation, which is rather surprisingly weak.

One principal university in Peru which could be serving the development programs of the present government to a much greater degree is the National Engineering University in Lima. The government of Peru in the 1960's has been moving forward rapidly on infra-structure construction and national industrial development.

But the leading engineering university in the country has partici-pated very little in these developments. Two different Mexican engineering professors, on separate occasions, visiting the Faculty of Civil Engineering at the National Engineering University, have observed that there is no organized program to enable the Univer-sity's advanced students and young faculty members to participate, during the summer months or on a training-internship basis, in the many public works projects underway all over Peru. In this connec-tion, Dr. Honey has an excellent proposal for the establishment of study-internship programs to draw carefully selected university students into the public service and to complement the internship in a public agency with a later opportunity for study abroad. In Peru, ONRAP would be performing a most significant service by taking the initiative in organizing such a program. It would, of course, have to secure the active cooperation of the major Peruvian universities and of key government officials and political leaders.

It seems to this writer that in the Peruvian setting the improve-ment of the quality of public administration depends as much as anything on a stimulation of interest among capable professional and technical personnel in *public* problems and their resolution. My impression is that there are many people in Peru at present—doctors, engineers, lawyers, businessmen, and others—who could make extraordinary contributions to government programs with minimal additional training but who have little interest in doing so. The universities are the institutions where, probably better than any-where else, dedication to public service can be stimulated or stifled.

This commentary should not be concluded without some concern being expressed about what seems to be a relative lack of interest on the part of ONRAP, which is the Peruvian government's central institute of public administration, in cooperation with the nation's *public* universities. These universities, by sheer force of numbers of students and of tradition, play and will continue to play a strategic role in the formation of Peru's political leaders and civil servants. While collaboration with these large, cumbersome, and complex universities is no easy task, failure to work with them in programs of public administration development is to risk not reaching many students who are likely to be most influential in the future of their country.

One public organization in Peru which has shown an exceptionally strong interest in the development of higher educational resources, in the field of study most related to its responsibilities, is the Banco Central de Reserva del Peru. Since 1961 the Bank has undertaken a series of extension activities aimed at increasing public understanding of Peruvian monetary institutions and policies and at strengthening the country's very limited human resources in the field of economics. The library of the Bank, which is probably the best economics library in the country, is open to the public, and many university economics students in Lima take advantage of the collection. A number of public and university librarians have also been invited to participate in a special training program organized by the Bank's library. The projected publication of a bulletin of abstracts of economic research being conducted in Peru promises to make an important contribution to economics documentation.

Each year the Bank offers intensive courses in economic theory and policy to a specially selected small group of outstanding fourth- and fifth-year university students from all over Peru. These courses are taught during the university summer vacations by a very capable group of young and dedicated economists on the Bank's staff, with some assistance from foreign economists working in Peru. Originally designed at least in part as a way of identifying and recruiting promising economists for the Bank's staff, the courses have developed into the best economics instruction offered in Peru.

The Bank's economists are also encouraged to teach on a part-time basis at universities in Lima, and five or six do so on a regular basis. One has also served on the Board of Advisers to the Institute of Economic Research of the University of San Marcos, and a second is currently consulting at Catholic University on curriculum reform and faculty development plans. Both of these economists have been trained at the doctorate level at Harvard, and the service they have provided is of the first order.

In August, 1966, the Bank held the first of what has become an annual two-week economics seminar for university professors throughout the country. These seminars deal intensively with one topic of economic theory and its applications and expose the professors to the most recent developments in economic analysis and instruction. It is hoped that through the seminars interest can be stimulated in economic research which is related to Peruvian development problems.

The Ford Foundation has approved matching support over a three-year period for the Bank's University Extension Program in Economics. One of the components of the agreement with the Foundation is the awarding of two-year graduate fellowships for study abroad in economics to the most outstanding students of the Bank's summer courses. Teaching/research assistantships would then be offered to the students when they return to enable them to work on their theses and to teach part time at a leading Peruvian university.

The Ford Foundation's primary interest in the project with the Peruvian Central Bank is the opportunity which it presents to improve university education in economics. A slightly varied program, however, could be developed in a number of fields to strengthen both governmental institutions and related university resources. In each case the fellowships for study abroad, and assistantships or internships of one sort or another, would be the central feature of the program. A significant contribution would certainly be made to public administration development in Peru if, as Dr. Honey proposes, each major technical assistance and development loan project of the important national and international aid agencies would include a training program similar to the one outlined above. The success of the Bank's University Extension Program has been in large part due to the exceptional qualities of a small group of dynamic, young, well-trained economists at the Bank. Unfortunately, such a cadre of leaders exists in very few of the public ministries in Peru. Consequently, training and study-internship programs must be carefully developed first with a few of the most promising public institutions and must be directed at developing these cadres. Scattering bright young interns and trainees indiscriminately among ministries would surely be fruitless.

CONCLUSION

The celebrated "revolution of rising expectations" throughout the less-developed world has put demands on governments which were unheard of fifty years ago. Until this "revolution" there has probably been a tendency for the efficiency of government bureaucracy to progress more or less in step with technological development and economic progress. When it was seen, however, that economic development could be promoted by conscious government policy and is not just a "given" in the scheme of things, and also as less-developed countries began to take advantage of important technological breakthroughs in other countries, a serious degree of discontinuity was introduced in the relative advancement of economic progress (real and apparent) and public administration development.

Just as it was fallacious to assume that economic development is not capable of being consciously promoted, so is it untrue that improvement in the quality of public administration must await the process of economic development. In fact, given the discontinuity which has developed between economic progress and aspirations, on the one hand, and the ability of governments to satisfy the aspirations on the other, explosive political situations have resulted; and it becomes particularly important that ways be found to enhance the effectiveness of public action.

Typically, the first deliberate attempts to improve the effectiveness of public action are addressed only at correcting deficiencies in the *techniques* of public administration: government budgeting, accounting, personnel policies, purchasing and disbursement procedures, tax collection, etc. But such attempts fall far short of the basic problems that are holding governments behind in the development process, at least in Latin America: the indifferent or negative attitudes which citizens have toward the public service and the extreme scarcity of high-level human resources in the public service.

The conclusions of this commentary on public administration development in Peru are certainly consistent with those reached explicitly or implicitly in the Honey essay. The really significant elements of public administration development are the whole array of institutions in the country which determine attitudes toward government and public problems, and the higher education institutions where both attitudes and important technical and professional skills are acquired simultaneously. From the vantage point of foreign assistance organizations, higher education and training has special relevance since it is here, much more than with the basic "attitude forming" agencies (families, churches, primary and secondary schools, etc.), that foreign assistance can be effective.

With respect to higher education in Peru, the social sciences and particularly an empirical approach to these disciplines, must certainly receive increased attention, as Dr. Honey suggests, if public administration development programs are to be successful. I doubt, however, that improving social science education as such will have much impact on public administration nor ultimately be successful per se, unless ways are found to introduce empirically oriented social science material into a *university* curriculum—as opposed to that of an isolated faculty. The social sciences do not really fit into the present framework of the Peruvian universities, primarily because the "social scientist" is not considered to have a profession. To gain an accepted place in the major universities in Peru, the social sciences must probably await reforms which will recognize the desirability of general education programs or liberal arts at the university level. The general studies programs at various planning stages in the universities of San Marcos, Trujillo, Arequipa, and Catholic University all have, in one form or another, the social or "human" sciences as one of four or five areas of concentration. Implementation of these or similar programs is a prerequisite to genuinely effective social science development in Peru.

What is probably even more important than strengthening the social sciences in the Peruvian universities, from the vantage point of public administration, is the necessity of deliberate promotion throughout the university of knowledge, constructive attitudes, and interest in public affairs. There are opportunities for the stimulation of such interest in virtually every faculty: medical students in matters of public health and population problems; law students in questions of tax reform and land tenure; engineering students in public works and industrial development; students of letters in problems of literacy and social psychology. These are only a few examples.

The University Extension Program in Economics of the Peruvian Central Bank is illustrative of how interest in a public institution can be promoted. In large part because of the success of this program, the Bank is held in high regard as a career opportunity by economics students. This kind of attraction of the best university graduates to public service seems to me to present the single most promising hope for public administration development in Peru.

Venezuela

GEORGE SUTIJA

Recent literature in international development underscores the fact that inefficient public administration constitutes a main stumbling block to economic and social progress in the underdeveloped world. Nowhere is this more evident than in Latin America. Although the nature of public administration differs slightly from country to country, all of the Latin countries seem to have had a number of characteristics in common, insofar as public service is concerned: inefficiency, corruption, poorly trained personnel, resistance to change, low prestige in society, etc. In recent years, however, distinctions in the quality in individual countries have occurred through the efforts of governments and the public to improve bureaucratic machinery by means of research in public affairs, training of personnel on different levels at home and abroad, legislative statutes, and implementation of administrative programs and projects.

In these efforts Venezuela has done comparatively well, especially when one understands the country's historical and social background and its long periods of dictatorship. For the first two decades of this century, until the discovery of the oil fields, Venezuela was considered a backwater of the Latin American world, and its society was typically traditional; it may well have been the least developed of all Latin American countries. During the first three decades of the twentieth century Venezuela was ruled by a quasi-illiterate dictator and for most of the next three decades by an assortment of military caudillos. The discovery of oil changed the economic situation rapidly, and this in turn created a favorable atmosphere for young political leaders to form political parties and establish a united democratic opposition to the dictators. The struggle was tough and long and culminated in the revolution of 1958, when the last dictator was overthrown and a democratic government began to rule the country.

The first president after 1958, Rómulo Betancourt, elected by direct vote, served his five-year mandate in full. His government had enormous problems to solve on many fronts, one of which was to improve the bureaucracy. It supported and organized several centers of research and training: the Commission on Public Administration and the School of Public Administration; the Foundation for Community Development and Municipal Improvement (COMUN); the Center for Studies of Development (CENDES); and the Institute of Advanced Studies of Administration (IESA). Support for these agencies has continued under the administration of President Raúl Leoni, elected in 1963.

These and associated developments are interesting to appraise in the light of the Honey essay which suggests strategies for public administration development. The essay is directed to a broad audience; it proposes certain specific actions which Latin American countries should undertake individually and regionally. The first proposal is for the establishment of a national council on public service for each country, and the role of this council is described in detail. Also proposed is a Latin American center for public affairs and a Latin American social science research council.

A social science research council similar to the one proposed by the Honey essay is already in the making. A conference of representatives of leading social science research centers of several Latin countries was held in Caracas in the fall of 1966. This conference was organized under the auspices of three leading centers: El Colegio of Mexico, Di Tella of Argentina, and CENDES from Central University in Venezuela, which also served as host. A second conference to be held in Bogotá in October, 1967, was scheduled. These efforts have been followed by a meeting in Chile of a smaller group of leading Latin Americans, including Felipe Herrera, Raúl Prebisch, Victor Urquidi, and Luis Lander, who have now taken the first steps to form a Latin American Council of Social Sciences. They elected an organizing committee with the intention that a council would be formally established at the Bogotá conference. This represents an important move for studies and research in the social sciences throughout Latin America, but what immediate impact it may have on the improvement of the social sciences is hard to predict. It is probable that it will be many years before results become evident.

The Honey proposal to establish a Latin American center for public affairs as a clearing house for public administration information, and to perform other functions similar to those carried on by the International Institute of Administrative Sciences is excellent and should be supported by one of the large inter-American organizations such as the Organization of American States or the Inter-American Development Bank. However, before a new regional organization is created, it would be wise to establish local national centers attached to important national agencies such as the national planning organization or a research center (e.g., CENDES) so that information collected and work done locally can be channeled to the proposed regional center.

At the present time the dearth of material on public affairs and the social sciences is unfortunately great. But in recent years there has been a rapid growth of relevant publications from many quarters, and it may now be time to establish information retrieval centers where such material can be managed and organized. In Venezuela there are two or three library centers which are already collecting such materials, but they face serious problems in finding and training professional staffs.

The most important suggestion the Honey essay makes is for the establishment of a national council on public service. Bringing such a council into being will be the hardest and most important of all the suggestions offered to implement. In a country such as Venezuela where the democratic life of the society started only eight years ago, where the government has a difficult time maintaining law and order, and is threatened by extreme elements from left and right, and where the business world looks with suspicion on people from the public sector and vice versa, it will take years of groundwork before a national council composed of citizens from many stratas can be formed.

Resistance to change in Latin America is very strong, based on long-established traditions, cultural backgrounds, particularized pressure group interests, and a myriad of psychological factors. There is opposition to proposals coming from outside the country as well as from those citizens within the country who clearly see that social changes must take place in order to improve the lot of the people.

Rapid economic growth in recent years has enlarged the bureaucracy of Venezuela. There are about 250,000 public employees in the country, of which about 100,000 are blue-collar workers. Their status in Venezuelan society is very low, and the word "bureaucracy" carries a strong derogatory connotation. José A. Silva Michelena in his study of the Venezuelan bureaucrat, states:

> Political, cultural, and economic elites unanimously evaluate bureaucrats negatively. Sizeable minorities among most groups share this negative view of government officialdom. Bureaucracy ranked eleventh among twelve occupational groups rated in terms of their contribution to the nation.[1]

There appears to be an assumption that bureaucrats are technically incompetent, ignorant, and lazy. A widely held view is that bureaucrats obtain their positions through family connections, or political influence, without having been properly trained and prepared for their jobs.

COMMISSION ON PUBLIC ADMINISTRATION

To improve the competence of Venezuelan public administration, the government in 1958 created the Commission on Public Administration, a Hoover-type commission with the prime target of bringing about administrative reform. Unfortunately, the Commission was from the beginning faced with great problems, and in nine years of existence its accomplishments have been modest. The Commission has been accused of having a partisan approach because one of its directors was an important leader of the governing party. Teams of foreign experts have been brought in, mostly from the United States, to advise on administrative reforms. Manuals, job classification specifications, and organizational charts have been developed, usually without antecedent study of the problems and needs of Venezuelan administration. There was a lack of confidence on the part of both those preparing the reform measures and the politicians who had guided them through the Congress, with the

---

[1] *Studying the Venezuelan Polity: Explorations in Analysis and Synthesis,* edited by Frank Bonilla and José A. Silva Michelena, Center for International Studies, M.I.T., Cambridge, Mass., Centro de Estudios del Desarrollo, Universidad Central de Venezuela, Caracas, Venezuela, May, 1966.

result that most proposals have not gotten much beyond the starting point. There has been strong opposition from the technical staffs of many ministries and, curiously enough, the strongest opposition has come from the best-run agencies. Nor has there been interest or concern on the part of the general public, or understanding of the reforms, even after over three years of discussion in Congress. Support from the President is essential to the Commission's success. In the beginning he was greatly concerned with issues of administrative reform, but subsequently he has turned his attention to more pressing problems, such as maintaining law and order and preserving democracy.

At first the Commission was primarily concerned with investigation and data accumulation, but in 1960 emphasis was shifted to implementation. The key areas of concentration were housing, agrarian reform, and sanitation and public works. Some of this work has been successful, but many recommendations of the Commission have never been carried out by the agencies. The original idea that the Commission's work would be strictly investigative and advisory, since, as it is attached to the President's office, its recommendations would automatically be carried through by executive action, has vanished. The Commission's prestige and power have declined. From the position of high stature it enjoyed in the beginning, it has now become a semi-independent and *un*influential agency. The clear evidence of this decline is that the budget of the Commission is lower now than it was initially.

Although the Commission's work fell short of early goals, there has been some impact on public administration in Venezuela. There now is an awareness in many quarters that administrative reform is urgent and that the need for better trained personnel in government agencies is of the utmost importance for the future development of the country. On the insistence of the Commission, many studies have been made within government agencies. Probably the most important effort has been in the Ministerio de Hacienda, where experts from the New York State government, under the auspices of the Agency for International Development, have assisted the budget office in reviewing and recommending steps to be taken to improve their operations. In so doing, a number of financial analysts now working in the different ministries have been given training.

Unless new administrative reform laws are passed by the Venezuelan Congress, the future of the Commission is uncertain. There are some indications that it could become a part of the government planning agency (CORDIPLAN).

THE SCHOOL OF PUBLIC ADMINISTRATION

The Commission, besides preparing the administrative reform bills and doing technical assistance work in different agencies, has also given attention to the training of personnel in public administration. In 1962, the School of Public Administration was formed, and the first course began in the fall of 1963. Primarily organized to offer in-service training for employees of the national government, the School is divided into four major parts. The first is the basic studies division, which offers courses to lower level personnel including office workers, secretaries, supply personnel, personnel for archives and files, and organization and methods analysts. The content of the courses is of a practical character designed to provide the students with training directly applicable to their jobs. Besides regular courses, the School offers short-term programs for such specialized personnel as executive secretaries and collective bargainers.

The second division, formed to train middle management level personnel offers courses in personnel administration, budget administration, accounting, and fiscal control. The third division offers the *bachillerato,* or high school degree program in public administration. Planned in cooperation with the Ministry of Education, the program is designed to provide a high school education for adults, especially persons presently working in the public service or planning to do so. The program runs for three years and covers many of the basic high school subjects plus public administration and organization and methods. The first graduates completed their work in the fall of 1966.

The fourth division is a research center created to undertake studies in social, economic, and political structures of Venezuela and to determine the conditions under which administrative reform is feasible and desirable in the Venezuelan environment. It was also hoped that the materials thus developed could be used in the School as teaching materials for different courses. Studies have been initi-

ated in such areas as government decentralization, capital investment in the public sector, and public attitudes regarding local
governments.

The staff of the School, consisting mainly of part-time instructors
from government agencies, has a high turnover rate, just as has
the Commission. From the beginning, the School, as well as the
Commission, lacked support on the part of the government and
especially from CORDIPLAN and the Ministry of Hacienda, two
principal planning agencies of the government. As a result, the
budget of the School is far below its needs. Unless the attitude of
the most important government agencies changes, the School can
never develop into an important training center in public administration. The School's leaders lack political influence and professional strength; the teaching staff is insufficiently trained or not
trained at all in public administration. Students sent to study abroad
for the purpose of building faculty competence do not always return to the School after their graduate training but accept more
attractive positions either in other government agencies or in private enterprise.

There has also been a lack of teaching materials and poor utilization of such as are available. The School unfortunately does not
have a precise and well-defined policy, but rather has tried to accomplish a very wide range of public administration training and
research endeavors. There has been little incentive on the part of
civil servants to invest their time and energy in studying at the
School. This results in a very high dropout rate from the courses
and a lack of interest and support on the part of the students and
the ministries who send them to the School. If the Commission and
the School are to survive, there is definitely a need for a new
and fresh approach. Most important is strong government support—
both moral and financial—for their work.

FOUNDATION FOR COMMUNITY DEVELOPMENT AND
MUNICIPAL IMPROVEMENT (COMUN)

While the Commission on Public Administration has suffered
from a lack of support from high levels of government, the reverse is true of the Foundation for Community Development and

Municipal Improvement (COMUN). The government, from CO-MUN's establishment in January, 1961, has supported this organization fully, providing it with influential and capable presidents and executive secretaries. Because the goal of the government is to bring about rapid economic and social improvement throughout Venezuela, its leaders immediately realized that this would be possible only through strengthening government operations at the municipal level, so that communities could handle their own affairs more effectively. For the first time in the history of Venezuela, the central government was more concerned with the development of the Venezuelan hinterland than with the capital of the country. Perhaps there was good political reason—the principal strength of the government party comes not from the capital city but from the peasants in small and medium-sized towns. At the same time, there was considerable threat from militant leftist guerilla activity, and the government was very much interested in strengthening the power of local and regional governments. The government was also interested in decentralizing the excessive power of the central government. These efforts have been successful and COMUN now plays a significant role. Its activities take three main directions: (a) technical assistance to municipalities, (b) financial assistance, and (c) community development programs.

Immediately after the establishment of COMUN, the Betancourt administration received a long-term loan of $30 million from the United States government which was made available on a re-loan basis to municipalities presenting sound public works projects (sewerage systems, streets, water supply, etc.), low-cost housing, school construction, and other economic development projects. Those funds have been matched by equal contributions to COMUN from the Venezuelan government. At about the same time, the Ford Foundation made a grant to COMUN to strengthen the capacity of municipalities in different aspects of administration. The Institute of Public Administration, New York, was the backstopping organization to bring a team of experts in planning, financing, legal, and cadastral services. Both programs have proved to be very successful, and through these combined efforts, COMUN has emerged as a viable national institution. It enjoys the high respect and confidence of municipalities throughout Venezuela. The mutual cooperation of the government, banks, and municipalities in developing housing and public works programs has been outstanding. Seminars and conferences have been held for hundreds of municipal officials and employees throughout the nation and have spurred the interest in techniques to improve performance. Through assistance from AID and the Creole Corporation, groups of municipal council presidents have been sent to the United States for one month of special training at the School of Public Administration of the University of Southern California. A national organic law for municipalities was prepared and before it was submitted to the national legislature for approval was discussed with many municipal officers. A number of municipal ordinances covering financing, budgeting, tax collection, industrial licensing, etc., have been prepared, and some of them have already been adopted. In this process, technical manuals have been written to assist municipal officers in their work and to serve as teaching materials in training courses. Correspondence courses have also been offered. Regional training centers throughout Venezuela have been established to provide training and technical assistance to municipalities, under contract arrangements. Cadastral work, on a pilot basis, was carried out in one city, and cadastral manuals have been prepared so that this work can be carried on in the future in many other cities. COMUN sent a number of its staff members for additional training abroad, especially to the United States, Puerto Rico, and Brazil, and these experts are returning to become permanent members of the COMUN staff.

COMUN established a professional library in the field of local government and community development, probably one of the best in Latin America. Through numerous training activities, research work, and implementation programs, COMUN gained enormous experience and is improving its work constantly. The very small staff of five years ago is now one of the best developed of any agency concerned with local municipal government throughout Latin America. COMUN's financial programs are well managed. Almost 15,000 housing units have been constructed so far with COMUN financial assistance. Total construction under COMUN auspices reached almost $100 million through loans from AID, local banks, and the government. COMUN is anticipating a grant from the United Nations Special Fund for further training programs and assistance to Venezuelan municipalities. The organization seems destined to continue to play a very important role in the economic and social development of Venezuela.

INSTITUTE FOR ADVANCED STUDIES OF ADMINISTRATION (IESA)

One of the important positive aspects of Venezuelan economic development is the genuine concern and interest on the part of the private sector of the community in national development. In 1962, a leading Venezuelan businessman and philanthropist launched a program called the Voluntary Dividend for the Community (*Dividendo*) with these basic goals: (a) to stimulate contributions of the business community to the solution of Venezuelan socio-educational problems; (b) to spur business corporations to pledge 2–5 per cent of their annual net profits to Dividendo-sponsored programs; (c) to enable Dividendo, either directly or through other agencies, to evaluate, endorse, and support existing organizations which have broad philanthropic objectives; (d) to establish for private agencies a central clearing house to collect statistics, furnish technical assistance and advice, and provide necessary services and funds; and (e) to provide a liaison between public and private agencies through collecting funds for national development programs. The business community responded favorably to this call, and the contributions for the programs reached almost $15 million in 1966.

At the same time, some Venezuelan business leaders have become concerned with the need of the national economy for highly trained and qualified administrators for both the private and public sectors. The Venezuelan economy has the highest growth rate in Latin America, and thanks to the nation's enormous natural resources, industry and commerce have expanded rapidly in recent years. Education of technical and managerial personnel to meet the needs of the economy has not kept pace with this development, however, and there is an acute shortage of competent and well-trained managers.

Venezuelan universities and other centers offer few opportunities for managerial training. Under the leadership of a director of the Creole Petroleum Company, an institute for advanced studies of administration is being created to offer young Venezuelans training similar to that given in U.S. graduate programs in public and business administration. The organizer of this effort, who had been the first director of the Venezuelan Commission of Public Administration, launched a campaign to obtain necessary support from the business community, international agencies, and the government to establish the new institute. Between 1964 and 1966 a large number of Venezuelan business firms had pledged over $3 million to the creation of the School. This response on the part of the private sector attracted the attention of CORDIPLAN, the government planning agency, and the municipal government of Caracas, as well as the Ford Foundation, all of which became interested in supporting the School. The municipal government of Caracas donated land where the facilities of the institute will be located, and plans are being developed for teams of visiting professors from leading U.S. schools of business and public administration to assist as teachers and advisers. The School's program will be at the postgraduate level. Several young Venezuelans, who will comprise the nucleus of the future faculty of the School, are already in the U.S. working toward their Ph.D.'s in business and public administration.

CENTER FOR STUDIES IN DEVELOPMENT (CENDES)
OF CENTRAL UNIVERSITY

The Center for Studies in Development (CENDES) was created in 1960 as a part of Central University of Venezuela. It is the nation's principal center for training and research in the social sciences, with special emphasis on development in Latin America. Although CENDES is part of Central University, and its director is directly responsible to the rector of the University, it was envisioned primarily as a research and training arm of the national planning agency (CORDIPLAN), from which it receives most of its funds. The objectives of CENDES are to study, analyze, and investigate the Venezuelan scene in its economic, social, and administrative aspects; to develop techniques related to planning and development of the country; to train technical personnel in the preparation and implementation of development plans at the postgraduate levels; to disseminate both theoretical and practical aspects of planning and implementation; to serve as a technical agency for the University Council for the development of science and humanities; and to serve as a consulting agency to institutions working in development fields.

CENDES' activities are divided into two parts: postgraduate training and research in the field of development. Postgraduate training serves to prepare experts to work in the planning agencies on a national, regional, and local level. The three different fields of specialization in which CENDES offers courses are regional economic planning, agricultural planning, and social planning. The first year of study consists of a basic course for all students. The second year is one of specialization. Admissions requirements for students are quite rigid; the School offers only day-time courses for full-time students. Adequate scholarships are offered to those who cannot finance their own studies. A number of the best students go on to further training overseas.

The second aspect of CENDES' activities is research conducted by its own personnel or in cooperation with international research centers and specialists brought to Venezuela. Of the research published thus far, the most important is a study on leadership and conflict and consensus in Venezuelan society, carried out in cooperation with the Center for International Studies of the Massachusetts Institute of Technology. This study, published in May, 1966, consists of several research projects undertaken by individuals or groups of researchers, who sought "through survey studies and other information concerning the power structure, political processes and characteristics of key groups in the population to determine the feasibility or relative social cost of these alternative strategies."

The fact that CENDES did research work in cooperation with M.I.T.'s Center for International Studies suggests the quality of the CENDES staff. The conflict and consensus study analyzes social change in Venezuelan leadership, the bureaucracy, among peasants, etc., and is certain to be regarded as a model for future studies throughout Latin America. Other CENDES studies have been in sanitation, industrial development, and community development. An important project now under consideration is concerned with Venezuelan urban problems, to be undertaken in association with the United Nations Special Fund.

CENDES was an intellectual creation of the late Chilean economist, Dr. Jorge Ahumada, whose able, vigorous, and imaginative leadership put CENDES into national and international prominence. His untimely death in the fall of 1965 deprived CENDES and the social sciences in Latin America of an outstanding man. He was the first director of CENDES and his deputy, Dr. Luis Lander, succeeded him as director.

CONCLUSION

Besides the centers described above, several universities have initiated courses in administration, and the Ministries themselves have developed in-service training programs. (Those organizations which have received the genuine support of the government and the public have done very well, whereas those that lack such support have had to struggle for survival.) But what is most important is that cadres of young, well-trained Venezuelans are becoming deeply involved in the affairs of their country and are gradually assuming responsible positions within the country's political and economic structure. Many have been trained in American universities, and their approach tends to be empirical and pragmatic. They are changing patterns and procedures and are helping to convert their society from a traditional to a modern one. It appears that these young men will in the future accomplish what Honey is proposing for the betterment of their national bureaucracy. With the private community interested in the problems of national development, and the deep concern of political leaders in strengthening public administration by means of training and research, it may well be possible in the future for young Venezuelans to form a council on public service—one of the main proposals advanced by the Honey essay for assuring national attention to public administration needs within individual countries.

Index

169